The
British Columbia
Cookbook

Jennifer Ogle • James Darcy • Jean Paré

Pictured on front cover Confit-style Salmon p. 24

The British Columbia Cookbook

Copyright © Company's Coming Publishing Limited

First Printing June 2012

Library and Archives Canada Cataloguing in Publication

The British Columbia cookbook / Eric Pateman ... [et al.].

(Canada cooks)

Includes index.

At head of title: Company's coming.

ISBN 978-1-897477-82-3

1. Cooking, Canadian--British Columbia style.

2. Cooking--British Columbia. 3. Cookbooks

I. Pateman, Eric, 1972- II. Series: Canada cooks series

TX715.6.B75 2012   641.59711   C2011-907089-8

Portions of this book were previously published by Lone Pine Publishing as *The British Columbia Seasonal Cookbook*, 2007. Company's Coming recipes contributed by Jean Paré: Prawn Bisque, Spaghetti Arcobaleno, Lemon Ginger Halibut, Kimchee Crab Cakes, Cranberry Bison Meatballs, Tamarind Vegetable Curry, Apple Pear Chutney, Blossom Cups with Jicama Shrimp Filling. Special thanks to Brad Smoliak for his Confit-style Salmon recipe, and to Lavoni Walker for her recipe and food styling for Smoked Salmon with Asparagus Salad.

Published by

Company's Coming Publishing Limited

2311 – 96 Street

Edmonton, Alberta, Canada T6N 1G3

Tel: 780-450-6223   Fax: 780-450-1857

www.companyscoming.com

We acknowledge the financial support of the Government of Canada through the Canada Book Fund for our publishing activities.

Printed in China

CONTENTS

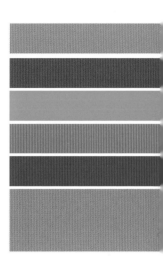

The Company's Coming Legacy

Jean Paré grew up with an understanding that family, friends and home cooking are the key ingredients for a good life. A busy mother of four, Jean developed a knack for creating quick and easy recipes using everyday ingredients. For 18 years, she operated a successful catering business from her home kitchen in the small prairie town of Vermilion, Alberta, Canada. During that time, she earned a reputation for great food, courteous service and reasonable prices. Steadily increasing demand for her recipes led to the founding of Company's Coming Publishing Limited in 1981.

The first Company's Coming cookbook, *150 Delicious Squares*, was an immediate bestseller. As more titles were introduced, the company quickly earned the distinction of publishing Canada's most popular cookbooks. Company's Coming continues to gain new supporters in Canada, the United States and throughout the world by adhering to Jean's Golden Rule of Cooking: Never share a recipe you wouldn't use yourself. It's an approach that has worked—millions of times over!

A familiar and trusted name in the kitchen, Company's Coming has extended its reach throughout the home with other types of books and products for everyday living.

Though humble about her achievements, Jean Paré is one of North America's most loved and recognized authors. The recipient of many awards, Jean was appointed Member of the Order of Canada, her country's highest lifetime achievement honour.

Today, Jean Paré's influence as founding author, mentor and moral compass is evident in all aspects of the company she founded. Every recipe created and every product produced upholds the family values and work ethic she instilled. Readers the world over will continue to be encouraged and inspired by her legacy for generations to come.

INTRODUCTION

British Columbia is blessed with abundant farmland, the vast waters of the Pacific Ocean, pristine inland lakes and streams, as well as the climate and conditions to produce a wide variety of food. Local farms produce meats, eggs, vegetables, fruits and grains. Artisans and small producers offer almost every imaginable food—from cheese, beer, wine and bread to preserves, ice cream and pies—all made from locally grown ingredients. The natural environment is also a rich food source, providing everything from freshwater fish to succulent berries to wild mushrooms.

Cioppino with Fennel and Saffron, p. 130

Food is a vital part of history and culture. It reflects a place and the people who live there. BC's food producers have a rich history that ties their origins to their present places, creating a unique and diverse culture. People from all over the world have settled in BC and brought their traditional foods with them. Their recipes have changed and adapted to the locally available resources. We like to say that in BC we taste the best ideas from around the world and make them our own using our amazing local ingredients.

In the past, if a food wasn't in season, we probably couldn't get it. The foods we ate changed depending on the time of year, and we had an intimate connection with our food and where it came from. Now fresh food can quickly travel from around the world to our dinner table. Wide selection and convenience are the great advantages of our modern world. The great disadvantage is that we have become disconnected from where our food comes from. We give little thought to how far it has had to travel and what financial, ethical or environmental costs the production of imported food may have.

Eating seasonally takes advantage of what locally grown foods are available. It supports the local economy, and it often provides us with fresher and tastier food. Perhaps most importantly, it connects us to the origins of our food. By speaking directly to food producers at such places as farmers' markets, U-pick farms and wineries, we learn not only the bounty of foods available at home, but also the value of the people involved in their production. We can even become food producers ourselves, by growing our own fruits and vegetables in our gardens or balcony planters.

With this book, we have created a resource of recipes that represent some of the best of what BC has to offer. Meat, fowl, eggs, cheese and wine are available all year and can be combined with seasonal foods that change throughout the year. Spring offers us tender asparagus and sweet, crisp peas. Summer brings many fresh fruits, wonderful to enjoy in pies, ice cream and smoothies. Fall's first frost sweetens parsnips, Brussels sprouts and Jerusalem artichokes. Winter warming comes in the form of roasted root vegetables and soups. It's all here, in the appetizers, salads, soups, main and side dishes, desserts and snacks that make up the seasons of this book.

Essential Ingredients

The following ingredients are used in many of the recipes in this book; special ingredients found in just one or two recipes are described where they are used. Some items are widely available, whereas others are best sought in gourmet, specialty food, health food or ethnic stores or obtained by mail order or the Internet.

Bay Leaves—Fresh leaves have such a different flavour that they are worth the effort to find. They are occasionally available at large grocery stores and can be specially ordered. In a well-sealed container in the fridge, they can last three or four months.

Coconut Milk—Use unsweetened coconut milk in cans. Naturally sweet, it is often better than cream in savoury dishes.

Garlic—Use fresh garlic! An Italian friend once told me that if you can't be bothered to peel and chop fresh garlic you shouldn't be allowed to use it!

Lemons and Limes—Use fresh! You can't compare the taste to concentrate.

Smoked Salmon and Asparagus Salad, p. 12

Grilled Asian Pears and Avocado Salad with Lemongrass and Garam Masala Vinaigrette, p. 124

Mayonnaise—It's always better homemade:

5 egg yolks

⅔ cup (150 mL) extra virgin olive oil

¼ cup (60 mL) good quality vinegar or juice of 1 lemon

pinch of sea salt to taste

• You need both hands free to make mayonnaise. Spread a damp cloth on your counter, nestle a medium-sized bowl in its centre and wrap it around base of bowl to keep it steady while you whisk.

• Whisk yolks, vinegar and salt in bowl until well combined and yolks have lightened in colour.

• Add oil, a drop at a time, whisking continuously until mixture emulsifies and thickens.

• When about half of oil has been added, add remaining oil in a slow, steady stream. Store, covered, in refrigerator for up to 5 days. You can thin your mayonnaise by lightly whisking in some water.

• Many people like to add mustard or fresh herbs to their mayonnaise. Adding minced garlic turns plain mayonnaise into aioli. Makes just over 1 cup (250 mL).

Mustard—Use good quality mustard for everything from sandwiches to dressings to sauces. When you are down to the last

Gnocchi in a Sorrel Sauce p. 106

few teaspoons clinging to the bottom of your mustard jar, add fresh lemon juice, olive oil, sea salt and fresh pepper for a yummy impromptu salad dressing. Just shake and enjoy.

Oil, Sesame—Use for a nutty flavour addition. Store it in the fridge.

Oil, Olive—Extra virgin olive oil is indispensable. Try olive oil from Italy, Spain or Greece.

Oil, Grape Seed—Use for higher heat cooking.

Pepper, Fresh—Please don't use pre-ground pepper; it has such poor flavour. A variety of peppercorns are available. Black or white can be used interchangeably in any of the recipes.

Salt—Great salt is the key to great cooking. Salt brings out the flavour in food. Sea salt, kosher salt, Celtic salt—choose a favourite. Better yet, get some of each. Using a better quality salt also means that you will use less, because the flavour is more intense. If you need to reduce salt even further for health reasons, use fresh herbs, various spices and flavour lifters, such as lemon juice, to maintain the flavour intensity while reducing the salt content.

Soy Sauce: Both tamari and shoyu are high quality, fermented and chemical-free "soy sauces" that are used to enhance flavour and impart a unique saltiness.

Stocks—Make homemade. Good quality stocks available in tetra packs are the best substitute. Miso, a fermented soybean paste, is another interesting alternative to stock, and it will keep in the refrigerator for several months. Stir it in 1Tbsp (15 mL) at a time until you have a rich, full flavour.

Vinegar, Apple Cider—Use when you need an all-purpose vinegar; organic, unrefined and unpasteurized has the best flavour.

Vinegar, Balsamic—Its unique flavour is great in everything from soups to sweets. Be sure to try BC's own balsamic such as Venturi Schulze of Okanagan Vinegar Brewery.

Measuring

Dry ingredients should be spooned into the measuring cup and levelled off with a knife or spatula.

Measurements are in both metric and imperial. Note that for butter, a pound is considered to be 454 g; for meat, vegetables, etc., a pound is 500 g.

Solids, including butter and most cheeses, are measured in dry-measure cups and liquids in liquid-measure cups.

Grilled Asparagus and Carmelis Chèvre Salad

Serves 4

BC, like other Canadian provinces, is dotted with artisan goat cheese producers. One to visit if you are in the Okanagan is nestled on a hillside outside of Kelowna overlooking the lake. Carmelis is a family-owned boutique dairy that produces a multitude of delicious goat cheeses for all tastes with milk from goats raised on its farm. One of its most popular styles of cheese is chèvre (French for "goat"), a tangy, fluffy and soft cheese synonymous with the French style of goat cheese. Most grocery store varieties are mild, moist and creamy and come in logs or cylinders, sometimes rolled in herbs or spices such as peppercorns, or coated with ash or edible leaves. As well, chèvre can be fashioned into other shapes, such as pyramids. Somewhat more piquant in taste than cheeses made with cow's milk, chèvre is often more easily digested by people with lactose intolerance; it also has twice the protein and one-third the calories. Goat's milk can also be made into other types of cheese, including feta, Gouda and Brie.

1 bunch (about 2 lb [1 kg]) asparagus, trimmed

splash of olive oil

sea salt and freshly ground pepper to taste

1 lb (500 g) package frozen peas, refreshed in boiling water, drained and cooled

1 cup (250 g) chèvre, crumbled

½ cup (125 mL) fresh mint, chopped

½ cup (125 mL) fresh basil, chopped

1 lime, cut into 4 wedges

Preheat barbecue to medium-high. Toss asparagus with olive oil, salt and pepper. Grill for 4 minutes, turning once. Set aside.

In a medium bowl, toss together peas, chèvre, mint and basil. Cut warm asparagus into bite-sized pieces and add to bowl. (Cut asparagus after because it is much easier to grill if left whole!) Toss and season again if needed. Divide among 4 plates and garnish each salad with a lime wedge.

Tip

Soft cheeses such as chèvre do not slice well—they often end up as a crumbled mess, half stuck to the knife. The easiest way to cut soft cheese is with taut dental floss. Just be sure to use unflavoured floss!

Tip

Allow cheese to come to room temperature for at least
30 minutes (longer for hard cheese or if the room is
particularly cold) before serving in order to enjoy its full
flavour and aroma. Portion cheese, if desired, while cold
and keep it wrapped so it doesn't dry out before you are
ready to serve.

Cipollini and Asiago Stuffed Morels

Serves 4 as an appetizer

The morel is a species of mushroom highly coveted by BC chefs. Known for their nut-like flavour and meaty texture, morels grow year after year on the same forested sites, preferring the company of ash trees, but they flourish in the years immediately following a forest fire. Since the Okanagan forest fire of 2003, the Okanagan Valley (along with other fire-prone regions of BC) has seen a bumper crop of these tasty jewels of the forest. When stuffed with sweet cipollini onions and salty Italian cheese, these mushrooms make a perfect spring appetizer.

1 Tbsp (15 mL) grape seed or canola oil

½ cup (125 mL) cipollini onion, peeled and quartered

1 lb (500 g) fresh morels; reserve 12 largest to stuff and chop the rest

¼ cup (60 mL) white wine

1 clove garlic, minced

¼ cup (60 mL) parsley, chopped

2 Tbsp (30 mL) chives, chopped

¼ cup (60 mL) grated Asiago cheese

2 to 3 Tbsp (30 to 45 mL) panko (see opposite)

sea salt and freshly ground pepper to taste

(continued on next page)

In a medium saucepan, heat oil over medium and sauté cipollini onions until they start to caramelize, about 5 minutes. Add chopped mushrooms and wine, and cook for about 5 minutes. Add garlic, cook for 2 to 3 minutes and remove pan from heat. Stir in parsley, chives, cheese, panko, salt and pepper. Stuff reserved mushrooms with filling.

For lime mayonnaise, stir together lime zest and mayonnaise. Set aside.

For breading, place flour, eggs and panko into separate bowls. Heat clarified butter in a saucepan over medium-high. Bread stuffed morels one at a time, dipping first in flour, then egg and finally panko. Cook mushrooms in butter until brown and crispy. Serve hot with lime mayonnaise.

If you can't find fresh morels, frozen ones will work well too.

Tip

To remove any unwanted critters hiding in the morels, soak the mushrooms in salted water for at least 1 hour.

Tip

To make clarified butter, melt unsalted butter slowly over low heat. Gradually, froth will rise to the top with a layer of clear golden oil in the middle and a layer of milk solids on the bottom. Clarified butter is the middle layer. Skim off the froth and carefully ladle out the clear oil, leaving out the milk solids.

Panko is a Japanese-style breadcrumb that is now popular enough to be widely available in most grocery stores (or visit an Asian specialty grocer). It is an ultra-white, extra-coarse breadcrumb that stays particularly crispy when fried.

Lime Mayonnaise

zest from 1 lime

½ cup (125 mL) mayonnaise

Breading

½ cup (125 mL) flour

3 eggs, lightly beaten

2 cups (500 mL) panko

1 cup (250 mL) clarified butter (see Tip)

Smoked Salmon and Asparagus Salad

Serves 4

This incredibly delicious salad offers the opportunity to use many amazing BC products, including fresh asparagus, cranberries, honey and—most importantly—smoked salmon! This West Coast delicacy is generally at the top of the list of items visitors like to take back home with them. We use cold smoked salmon in this recipe, or lox as it is sometimes called, which is salmon that is cured but not cooked so it has a unique flavour and texture. Smoked salmon is also available as hot smoked, jerky, Indian candy or even Tandoori nuggets. If you're not already familiar with some of these products, make sure you try them the next time you are at your local fish counter.

¼ cup (60 mL) coarsely chopped dried sweetened cranberries

1 Tbsp (15 mL) drained and chopped capers

2 tsp (10 mL) honey

2 tsp (10 mL) balsamic vinegar

1 clove garlic, minced

2 Tbsp (30 mL) olive oil

sea salt and freshly ground pepper

1 bunch (about 2 lb [1 kg]) asparagus, trimmed

5 oz (150 g) cold smoked salmon slices

⅓ cup (75 mL) crème fraîche (see Tip)

1 large ripe avocado, peeled and sliced

chives and dill

Combine cranberries, capers, honey, vinegar, garlic, olive oil, salt and pepper in a small saucepan. Stir over medium heat until warm. Let stand for 15 minutes to allow cranberries to soften.

Blanch asparagus in a large saucepan of boiling, salted water for about 2 minutes or until bright green; drain. Immediately place asparagus in a bowl of ice water. Let stand about 10 minutes or until cool; drain. Return asparagus to same bowl. Add cranberry dressing and toss to combine. Arrange asparagus on 4 serving plates; drizzle with dressing. Top with smoked salmon, some crème fraîche, avocado, more crème fraîche and smoked salmon. Garnish with chives and dill, if desired.

Tip

If you can't find crème fraîche, use sour cream instead.

Spring, coho and sockeye salmon have a higher fat content than other species of salmon and so have the best flavour when smoked.

Prawn Bisque

Serves 6

Elegant and rich-tasting prawn bisque is most satisfying when sampled in small portions. When choosing the prawns for this dish, make sure they come from a reputable fish monger, that they are fresh and most importantly that they come from a sustainable source. Side stripe or spot prawns are usually good choices. Ocean Wise, a conservation program created by the Vancouver Aquarium, helps consumers be sure that their seafood purchases are sustainable. The Ocean Wise logo next to an item on a menu or in a display case means that particular item was harvested in an environmentally sound manner and is therefore a responsible, ocean-friendly choice.

1 Tbsp (15 mL) butter
6 uncooked medium prawns (peeled and deveined), tails intact

¼ cup (60 mL) finely chopped celery

¼ cup (60 mL) finely chopped carrots

¼ cup (60 mL) finely chopped shallots

3 oz (85 g) uncooked prawns (peeled and deveined), chopped

2 oz (55 g) tomato paste

½ cup (125 mL) whipping cream

¼ cup (60 mL) dry white wine

½ tsp (2 mL) chopped fresh tarragon

6 fresh tarragon leaves

Melt butter in a saucepan on medium heat. Add first 6 prawns and cook until pink. Transfer to a plate and set aside.

Add celery, carrots and shallots to same saucepan and cook for about 8 minutes until softened.

Stir in chopped prawns, tomato paste, whipping cream wine and tarragon. Simmer, covered, on medium-low for 20 minutes or until reduced by a third. Carefully process with hand blender or in a blender until smooth (see Tip).

Pour into 6 small serving cups and place 1 shrimp and 1 tarragon leaf over each cup of soup. Serves 6.

Tip

Follow manufacturer's instructions for processing hot liquids.

Remarkably succulent and sweet, spot prawns are caught with pots, widely agreed to be the most sustainable fishing method. Pots have few environmental impacts and hardly any "bycatch."

Wild Mushroom Soup with Herb Oil

Serves 6

Foraging for mushrooms is a pleasant and secretive pastime for many BC residents. The locations of the "best spots" for mushroom hunting are rarely disclosed and are spoken of in hushed tones, even within the family. The pine mushroom is the only species known to have been traditionally eaten by the First Nations of BC, and only by the Nlaka'pamux (Thompson River) and Stl'atl'mx (Lillooet) peoples. In the early 20th century, Japanese immigrants began to collect the pine mushroom *(matsutake)* for consumption and for sale. Today, the prized selections for both commercial and home foragers include morels, chanterelles, lobster and pine mushrooms, and BC's multimillion-dollar wild-mushroom industry ships to mushroom lovers all over the world.

3 cups (750 mL) fresh, cleaned wild mushrooms, such as chanterelles, lobster or morels

2 Tbsp (30 mL) olive oil

¼ cup (60 mL) unsalted butter, divided

1 large yellow onion, diced

2 large Yukon Gold potatoes, diced

¼ cup (60 mL) dry sherry

1 *bouquet garni* of parsley, thyme and bay leaf

3 dried juniper berries, bruised

4 cloves garlic, minced

8 cups (2 L) chicken or vegetable stock

1 cup (250 mL) heavy cream (32%)

(continued on next page)

Slice mushrooms into even-sized pieces and sauté in batches in a large pot with olive oil and ⅛ cup (30 mL) of butter until nicely browned. Remove mushrooms and set aside.

In same pot, melt remaining butter and add onions and potatoes. Sauté until golden, then deglaze with sherry. Add *bouquet garni*, juniper berries, garlic, sautéed mushrooms and stock. Bring to a boil, then immediately reduce heat to a simmer and cook until liquid is reduced by a third.

Add cream, bring almost to a boil and remove from heat. Remove *bouquet garni*. Purée soup in a blender until smooth. Serve hot, garnished with herb oil (see opposite).

Tip

To make a *bouquet garni,* simply wrap the herbs in cheesecloth and tie it shut to form a tidy bundle that can be easily extracted from the soup before serving.

Warning

Because some mushrooms contain deadly toxins, eat only mushrooms positively identified as edible.

Combine herbs and oil in a medium saucepan over medium heat until oil begins to sputter. Set aside to cool to room temperature. Purée mixture in a blender, then let sit for 1 hour. Strain mixture through a double layer of large coffee filters wrapped in cheesecloth. Allow plenty of time to strain mixture; do not press on solids or you risk making oil cloudy. Store in fridge for up to 2 weeks.

Tip

If suitable fresh wild mushrooms are not available, you can use half the quantity of dried wild mushrooms. Reconstitute them in hot water or stock for about 10 minutes. Add enough liquid to cover, using a small plate to keep them submerged. Save the liquid to add to your soup; it will be full of great mushroom flavour.

Herb Oil

1½ bunches of fresh assorted seasonal herbs such as parsley, oregano, thyme and rosemary, chopped

1 cup (250 mL) grape seed oil

Salt Spring Island Lamb with Mustard Spaetzle

Serves 4

So renowned is the taste and texture of Salt Spring Island lamb that many visitors to British Columbia ask for it by name. Even Queen Elizabeth is said to prefer it to lamb from any other corner of her Commonwealth. What makes Salt Spring Island lamb so unique? Perhaps it is the salt water from the ocean that travels inland on the wind to settle on the grass where the sheep graze. Or the rich, grainy diet the sheep and lambs are fed. It could just be the laid-back island lifestyle into which the lambs are born. Luckily for us locals, the lamb is available at Granville Island and through other top-quality butchers and restaurateurs.

2 x 1½ lbs (750 g) lamb racks, frenched (see Tip)

2 Tbsp (30 mL) extra virgin olive oil

sea salt and freshly ground pepper

1 clove garlic, minced

1 cup (250 mL) fresh parsley, chopped

2 Tbsp (30 mL) *each* fresh thyme and rosemary, chopped

¼ cup (60 mL) breadcrumbs

¼ cup (60 mL) Dijon mustard

(continued on next page)

Place a heavy-bottomed pan over medium-high heat. Brush lamb with oil and season with salt and pepper. Sear lamb until brown on all sides. Remove from heat and let sit 15 minutes.

Preheat oven to 450° F (230° C). Mix garlic and herbs together in a bowl with breadcrumbs. Place lamb on a small, rimmed baking sheet; brush Dijon mustard on rounded side of lamb. Divide breadcrumb mixture evenly over chops, covering mustard to form a crust. Bake for 10 to 15 minutes for medium-rare. Let rest 5 to 10 minutes before cutting into chops. Serve with spaetzle.

For spaetzle, bring a large pot of salted water to a boil. Set a bowl of ice water near pot. Sift flour and salt together. Whisk together eggs, milk and Dijon mustard and pour into flour, stirring to make a smooth batter. Using a spaetzle maker or food mill, drop batter into boiling water. When spaetzle come to surface, transfer them to ice water with a slotted spoon. Repeat until all batter is used. As they cool, remove spaetzle from water and place in sieve to drain. To reheat spaetzle, toss them in hot butter or sauce—or fry them over medium heat until golden.

Tip

Frenching is a technique where the rib bones of the rack of lamb are scraped clean of skin, meat and sinew using a very sharp knife and kitchen shears. If you don't feel up to this operation, ask your butcher to do it. Racks of lamb already frenched are sometimes available in the grocery store.

Spaetzle or spätzle ("little sparrow") are German dumplings very similar to pasta. They are served as a side dish and are common fare, especially in southern Germany and the Alsace region. Spaetzle makers are available at specialty food shops, department stores and German markets (where you will likely find a good one for a reasonable price).

Spaetzle

1¼ cups (310 mL) flour

1 tsp (5 mL) sea salt

3 eggs

⅓ cup (75 mL) milk

1 Tbsp (15 mL) grainy Dijon mustard

Spaghetti Arcobaleno

Serves 6 to 8

This dish features an attractive *arcobaleno* (Italian for "rainbow") of fresh, flavourful ingredients in a delicious light sauce. You can mix it up a little by changing the vegetables according to what is locally and seasonally available. We've chosen fresh asparagus or zucchini to give the recipe a taste of spring. Feel free to add olives or capers to give it a true Mediterranean feel. Garnish with shaved Parmesan cheese and small basil leaves.

8 oz (250 g) spaghetti

1 tsp (5 mL) olive oil

1 lb (500 g) salmon fillets, skin and any small bones removed

2 cups (500 mL) halved grape tomatoes

1½ cups (375 mL) chopped yellow pepper

½ cup (125 mL) dry white wine

½ cup (125 mL) sun-dried tomato pesto

¼ tsp (1 mL) salt

2 cups (500 mL) chopped fresh asparagus or zucchini (1 in [2.5 cm] pieces)

½ cup (125 mL) coarsely chopped fresh basil

1 Tbsp (15 mL) lemon juice

1 tsp (5 mL) grated lemon zest (see Tip)

¼ tsp (1 mL) pepper

(continued on next page)

Cook pasta according to package directions. Drain.

Heat olive oil in a large skillet on medium. Add fillets and cook for about 4 minutes per side until fish flakes easily when tested with a fork. Transfer to a plate. Cover to keep warm.

Add grape tomatoes, yellow pepper, wine, pesto and salt to same skillet and bring to a boil. Cook for about 10 minutes, stirring occasionally, until yellow pepper is tender.

Stir in asparagus or zucchini and pasta. Cook, covered, for about 1 minute until asparagus or zucchini is tender-crisp. Transfer to a large serving bowl. Break up salmon pieces and add to pasta mixture. Add basil, lemon juice, lemon zest and pepper, and toss until everything is nicely coated.

Tip

When a recipe calls for grated zest and juice, it's easier to grate the fruit first, then juice it. Be careful not to grate down to the pith (white part of the peel), which is bitter and is best avoided.

Homemade Pasta

Mix flour and eggs on low speed in a heavy-duty electric mixer until mixture has a coarse, crumbly look, like corn meal. Add water in small quantities until the mixture starts to hold together. Switch to the dough hook on the mixer, or knead by hand 7 to 10 minutes. Dough should not be sticky or in separate pieces. Add a little more liquid if needed, or a little more flour if sticky. Cover with plastic wrap and let dough rest 15 to 30 minutes. Roll through a pasta machine according to the manufacturer's instructions.

To cook, make sure water is at a full boil and very well salted. Fresh pasta cooks very quickly and will rise to the top of the water when done. Drain in a colander and do not rinse.

Homemade Pasta

1½ cups semolina flour

2 eggs

2 to 3 tsp lukewarm water

Lemon Ginger Halibut

Serves 6

Canada is now home to two artisan sake makers (one on Granville Island in Vancouver and one in the distillery district in Toronto). With the influence of Japanese cuisine on a Canadian dish, this recipe is the perfect opportunity to sip some sake with your dinner guests while the halibut cooks to moist, flaky perfection. Savour the aroma of lemon and ginger rising in the air. You're just moments away from experiencing the Asian-inspired flavours mingling on the grill.

¼ cup (60 mL) sake

3 Tbsp (45 mL) lemon juice

2 Tbsp (30 mL) brown sugar, packed

1 Tbsp (15 mL) canola oil

1 Tbsp (15 mL) finely grated ginger root

1 Tbsp (15 mL) soy sauce

2 cloves garlic, minced

2 tsp (10 mL) grated lemon zest (see Tip, p. 20)

½ tsp (2 mL) chili paste (sambal oelek)

6 halibut fillets (about 1 inch [2.5 cm] thick), about 4 to 5 oz (115 to 140 g) each

1 Tbsp (15 mL) finely chopped green onion

Combine sake, lemon juice, brown sugar, oil, ginger, soy sauce, garlic, lemon zest and chili paste in a large resealable freezer bag.

Add fillets and chill for 30 minutes. Drain marinade into a saucepan and simmer on medium-low until slightly thickened. Grill fillets on direct medium heat for about 4 minutes per side, brushing with thickened marinade, until fish flakes easily when tested with a fork.

Sprinkle with green onion before serving.

Pacific halibut are the largest flatfish in the Pacific Ocean; they can weigh up to 700 pounds (318 kilograms) and can grow to 9 feet (2.75 metres) long. The oldest halibut on record was 55 when it was caught, but the average lifespan for these fish is 25 years.

Confit-style Salmon

Serves 4

Traditional confits involve cooking meat such as duck in fat, but this recipe infuses the salmon with a great flavour that it acquires by marinating in the fridge overnight. You can cook the salmon right on the grill or in a cast iron skillet. Wild salmon from Campbell River, on Vancouver Island, is the best in this recipe.

4 x 8 oz (250 g) salmon fillets or steaks

2 cups (500 mL) extra-virgin olive oil

2 Tbsp (30 mL) chopped fresh basil

2 Tbsp (30 mL) chopped fresh parsley

2 Tbsp (30 mL) chopped fresh oregano

salt and pepper

freshly squeezed lemon juice

lemon wedges

Mix oil and herbs together in a medium bowl and season with salt and pepper. Place salmon in a baking dish and pour olive oil–herb mixture over the fish, flipping to coat both sides of the fish. Cover and refrigerate overnight.

Preheat the barbecue to medium-high and grease the grills well. Remove the fish from the olive oil and herb mixture; wipe as much oil from the salmon as possible. Grill fish, flesh-side down first, for 5 minutes per inch (2.5 cm) of thickness, or until desired doneness. Flip fish partway through.

To serve, squeeze lemon juice on the salmon and garnish with lemon wedges.

Cast Iron Method

Heat a cast iron skillet over high heat until a wisp of smoke curls up from pan. Place fish flesh-side down, and cook for 5 minutes. Flip and cook an additional 5 minutes, or until desired doneness. Serve as described above.

Potato Frittata

Serves 4

Potatoes are a popular kitchen staple because they are cheap, easy to cook, available year-round and tasty, making them a comfort food that adapts well to many recipes. Amazingly, the average Canadian eats about 163 pounds (74 kilograms) of potatoes per year. In BC, potatoes are grown mostly in the Lower Mainland, the Kootenays, the Okanagan and Vancouver Island. Derived from the Italian word *fritto* ("fried"), a frittata is an open-faced omelette made with cheese and other ingredients mixed into the eggs. It is a classic Italian dish traditionally served on Easter Day. Incorporating potatoes into this breakfast dish makes it an especially satisfying and comforting one-dish meal.

2 Tbsp (30 mL) butter

3 onions, sliced

2 medium Yukon Gold potatoes, peeled, cooked and sliced

8 eggs

¾ cup (175 mL) cream or milk

sea salt and freshly ground black pepper

½ cup (125 mL) Salt Spring Island chèvre cheese (or aged Cheddar cheese, grated)

1 Tbsp (15 mL) fresh thyme, chopped

Preheat broiler to 500° F (260° C). Melt butter in a 9 in (23 cm) nonstick, ovenproof pan over low heat. Add onions and sauté, stirring occasionally, for 10 to 15 minutes until onions are golden brown. Add potato slices and cook until starting to brown, about 5 minutes. Whisk eggs, cream or milk, salt and pepper in a bowl to combine. Pour egg mixture over onions in pan and sprinkle with cheese and thyme. Cook frittata for 5 to 6 minutes, until almost set. To finish cooking, place frittata under broiler for 1 minute. Cut into wedges and serve along with your breakfast favourites.

Potatoes are the most widely grown vegetable in the world. In BC, more potatoes are grown than any other vegetable.

 The Yukon Gold potato, now the favourite of chefs around the world for its texture, flavour and tempting golden flesh, was bred by Canadian Gary Johnston and his colleagues at the University of Guelph in the 1960s.

Braised Swiss Chard

Serves 4 as a side dish

With its bright red stalks and dark green leaves, this cool-climate lover is an ideal BC vegetable because it can withstand frost, and when planted in early spring, it is usually ready to eat within four to six weeks. It also rivals spinach as a great leafy green because, unlike spinach, it contains no oxalic acid, so the minerals it contains are more readily digestible. Chard is a kind of beet grown for its leaves rather than its roots. It packs a huge amount of vitamin A and is naturally high in sodium—1 cup (250 mL) contains 313 mg. This is the perfect spring vegetable because the tips are very tender and it offers a much different taste at this time of the year than in fall, when it is typically consumed. Try using it raw in a salad!

2 small red onions, chopped

1 Tbsp (15 mL) butter

2 lbs (1 kg) chard leaves, stems removed

¼ cup (60 mL) white wine

sea salt and freshly ground pepper to taste

Sauté onions in butter over medium heat in a large pan until nearly softened and lightly browned, about 8 to 10 minutes.

Meanwhile, clean chard leaves (see Tip) and slice into ribbons. Add chard leaves and wine. Cook rapidly, stirring frequently, until chard is wilted and liquid has evaporated, about 5 minutes.

Season with salt and pepper.

Tip

To clean chard, simply swish in cool water and pat dry. The stems and leaves are both edible but should be cooked separately because the stems take longer to cook.

Chard can be used instead of spinach or kale in your favourite recipes.

The photo below shows a simple presentation with beef kebobs.

Sourdough Hotcakes

Makes about 1 dozen

The first leavened breads rose through the action of yeast naturally occurring on the grains and in the air. Before the advent of modern yeast packaging methods, people wanting to bake bread would keep a "starter" containing a proven yeast strain. Prospectors in the San Francisco Gold Rush discovered that their starters were unusually tangy, and the term "sourdough" was born. During a time when food was even more important than money, sourdough was extremely valuable to these prospectors; they used it to feed themselves and their dogs, and the starter was even used to tan hides. It is still popular as a leavening agent today, used by well-known bakeries such as La Baguette et L'echalote and Terra Breads at Granville Island.

Quick Sourdough Starter

1 cup (250 mL) water

1 cup (250 mL) unbleached flour

½ tsp (2 mL) active dry yeast

Sourdough Hotcakes

2 cups (500 mL) sourdough starter (see above or opposite)

1½ cups (375 mL) unbleached or whole wheat flour

2 Tbsp (30 mL) sugar, maple syrup or honey

3 Tbsp (45 mL) oil

2 eggs

½ tsp (2 mL) sea salt

1 tsp (5 mL) baking powder

1 tsp (5 mL) baking soda, diluted in 1 Tbsp (15 mL) warm water

(continued on next page)

For starter, the night before you plan to make hotcakes, mix water, flour and yeast well and set out on a countertop in a draft-free area, allowing starter time to develop its characteristic sour taste. Remaining starter can be left on counter for future use; it is best stored at 65 to 77° F (18 to 25° C). To strengthen and "feed" starter, add ¼ cup (60 mL) water and ½ cup (125 mL) flour every second day.

For hotcakes, preheat griddle or pan to medium-high heat. Mix all ingredients except baking soda together. Gently fold in baking soda and cook cakes right away so as to not lose baking soda's leavening effect. Serve hot with your favourite condiments.

Old-fashioned Sourdough Starter

Boil unpeeled potatoes until they fall apart. Remove skins. Mash potatoes in a non-metallic bowl, adding water as needed to make a rich, thick liquid, about 2 cups (500 mL). Add sugar, flour and yeast, beating until smooth, and let stand for 1 week. Feed starter as described opposite for quick starter.

Old-fashioned Sourdough Starter

2 large potatoes

2 cups (500 mL) water

3 Tbsp (45 mL) sugar

1⅔ cups (400 mL) unbleached flour

½ tsp (2 mL) active dry yeast

Apple Cranberry Cinnamon Buns

Makes 12

Cinnamon rolls are a North American and northern European tradition, with entire stores in malls now dedicated to selling these sweet, sticky pastries. However, the best cinnamon rolls are the ones that come straight out of your oven, filling the house with the incomparable homeyness of baked bread and cinnamon. This variation of the traditional roll incorporates two of BC's best-known fruits: Granny Smith apples and Fraser Valley cranberries. Their tartness counters all the sugar and icing plus lends a local flavour. Served warm on a Sunday morning, these make the perfect weekend brunch treat.

Dough

¼ cup (60 mL) warm water

1 Tbsp (15 mL) active dry yeast

¼ cup (60 mL) sugar, *divided*

2¼ cups (560 mL) flour

½ cup (125 mL) buttermilk, room temperature

1 tsp (5 mL) salt

2 egg yolks

¼ cup (60 mL) unsalted butter, softened

Filling

½ cup (125 mL) dried cranberries

2 Granny Smith apples, peeled and chopped

⅓ cup (75 mL) brown sugar

1 tsp (5 mL) cinnamon

1 tsp (5 mL) cardamom

2 Tbsp (30 mL) unsalted butter, melted and cooled slightly

For dough, sprinkle yeast over warm water with 1 tsp (5 mL) sugar and let stand until foamy, 5 to 10 minutes. Add remaining sugar, flour, buttermilk, salt and egg yolks, and stir until well combined. Transfer mixture to an electric mixer with a dough hook and beat in butter, a few pieces at a time, on medium speed until smooth and elastic, about 5 minutes. Scrape dough from side of bowl and cover bowl with plastic wrap. Set bowl in a warm place for 1 hour or until dough has doubled in size.

For filling, stir together cranberries with apples in a small bowl. In a separate bowl, stir together brown sugar, cinnamon and cardamom.

Grease a 9 x 13 in (23 x 33 cm) baking pan. Transfer dough onto a floured surface and roll out into a 16 x 12 in (40 x 30 cm) rectangle. Brush dough with melted butter, leaving an unbuttered ½ in (12 mm) border on long sides. Sprinkle fruit filling evenly over buttered area and then sprinkle sugar mixture evenly over filling. Roll up shorter side of dough, like a jelly roll, and pinch to seal edge firmly. Cut into 12 even pieces and arrange, cut sides down, in baking pan. Cover loosely with plastic wrap and let buns rise in a warm place for 45 to 50 minutes or until they have doubled in size.

While buns are rising, preheat oven to 350° F (175° C). Bake buns in middle of oven until golden, about 25 minutes. Transfer buns to a rack and cool slightly before serving.

Since 1999, Sweden has celebrated National Cinnamon Bun Day on October 4 each year.

Nanaimo Bars

Makes 12 squares

Nanaimo is a picturesque community on central Vancouver Island. The Nanaimo District Museum receives so many inquiries into the origins of the Nanaimo bar that it is considering developing an exhibit in honour of this sinful treat. There are at least three similar bar recipes from the early 1950s. One, called "chocolate slice," appeared in *The Women's Auxiliary to the Nanaimo Hospital Cook Book* (1952); a second, published in the Vancouver Sun, was called "Nanaimo Bars"; a third version, "Mrs. Gayton's Bars," was printed in a 1955 cookbook from St. Aidan's United Church in Victoria. There is even a place in Nanaimo that has taken decadence to a whole new level with its "Deep Fried Nanaimo Bar."

Layer 1

½ cup (125 mL) butter

¼ cup (60 mL) sugar

2 Tbsp (30 mL) cocoa

1 egg

2 cups (500 mL) graham cracker crumbs

1 cup (250 mL) shredded coconut

½ cup (125 mL) toasted, chopped nuts of your choice

1 tsp (5 mL) pure vanilla extract

Layer 2

¼ cup (60 mL) half and half cream (10 to 18%)

2 Tbsp (30 mL) custard powder

3 Tbsp (45 mL) butter

1 tsp (5 mL) pure vanilla extract

2 cups (500 mL) sifted icing sugar

(continued on next page)

Layer 1

Soften butter in a double boiler. Add sugar, cocoa and egg and then heat until slightly thickened. Stir in rest of ingredients, and press mixture into a 9 inch (23 cm) square pan. Chill for 15 minutes.

Layer 2

Mix ingredients together and spread evenly over first layer. Chill for 15 minutes.

Layer 3

Melt chocolate and butter together until smooth and spread over second layer. Chill for 15 minutes. Score top with a sharp knife to make 12 squares, then cut and serve or store in an airtight container for up to 1 week.

Espresso Nanimo Bars

Add 2 tsp (10 mL) of instant espresso powder and 2 Tbsp (30 mL) of heavy cream (32%) to second layer. Once third layer has been spread, stud centre of each square with a chocolate-covered coffee bean. Chill, cut and serve.

Pistachio Ginger Nanaimo Bars

(featured in photo) Use ½ cup (125 mL) of chopped, unsalted pistachios as nuts in first layer. When second layer is cool, spread 1 cup (250 mL) of finely diced candied ginger over it, then pour third layer over top. Chill, cut and serve.

Layer 3

5 oz (140 g) semi-sweet chocolate

2 Tbsp (30 mL) butter

Rhubarb Pie with a Meringue Crust

Serves 6

Rhubarb is one of those things you either love or hate—there doesn't seem to be any middle ground on the subject. For early pioneers, the robust and hardy rhubarb plant supplied essential vitamins and minerals in spring before any berries ripened. Indigenous to Asia, rhubarb was first brought to Europe for its medicinal qualities. Huge plantations were soon established in Oxfordshire and Bedfordshire, England, where they still grow today. Officially recognized in Europe as a food, rhubarb was known as "pie plant" because it was most often presented as a pie filling and in other desserts. It was the English who brought the first rhubarb to Canada. This recipe offers a nice balance between the tart rhubarb and the sweet meringue crust.

1 cup (250 mL) sugar

3 Tbsp (45 mL) flour

1 tsp (5 mL) cinnamon

2 lbs (1 kg) rhubarb, frozen or fresh

Meringue

⅓ cup (60 mL) sugar

1 Tbsp (15 mL) cornstarch

5 egg whites

½ tsp (2 mL) cream of tartar

1 x 9 in (23 cm) pie crust, prebaked (or see p. 80 for Great Pie Crust)

Mix sugar, flour and cinnamon in a large bowl. Slice rhubarb into 1 in (2.5 cm) pieces, add to flour–sugar mixture and mix until well coated. In a saucepan over medium heat, cook rhubarb until it is soft and thickened, about 10 minutes. Let cool for at least 30 minutes.

For meringue, mix sugar and cornstarch in a small bowl. In another bowl, beat egg whites with an electric mixer until foamy. Add cream of tartar and beat in sugar–cornstarch mixture, 1 Tbsp (15 mL) at a time, until egg whites are stiff and glossy.

Pour cooled rhubarb filling into prepared pie crust and spoon meringue gently on top. Bake meringue-topped pie at 350° F (175° C) for 10 to 12 minutes until meringue is slightly golden.

Don't eat the plant's leaves—they're poisonous.

 *A member of the buckwheat family, rhubarb is closely related to sorrel. Although rhubarb is technically a vegetable, the stems are used as a fruit in most recipes.*

Maple Vanilla Cocktail

Serves 1

A perfect Vancouver day (rain or shine) involves outdoor activity on one of our mountains, at the beach or in Stanley Park and a coffee-based drink. With a coffee house (or two) on almost every city block, Vancouverites love their grande, non-fat, extra-hot, double-shot, half-sweet, extra-foam lattes. This recipe takes our early morning habit and turns it into a delectable evening treat. For this recipe, try using a local roaster such as Salt Spring Coffee Company, purveyors of certified organic, fair trade, shade-grown coffees from around the world

1 oz (30 mL) espresso

1 oz (30 mL) Sortilège

1 oz (30 mL) vodka

½ oz (15 mL) heavy cream (32%)

½ oz (15 mL) vanilla syrup

ice

Add espresso, Sortilège, vodka and cream to a cocktail shaker and shake. Strain into a martini glass filled with ice.

Tip

The ice is added last so that the hot espresso doesn't melt it and water down the martini.

Sortilège is a unique blend of Canadian whisky and maple syrup, made in Québec. Reminiscent of maple toffee, this subtly sweet liqueur balances the potent headiness of whisky with the distinctive maple sweetness. The word sortilège *means "sorcery" in French.*

Okanagan Apple and Quinoa Salad

Serves 6 as a main-course salad

Kelowna Land and Orchard (KLO) Company is one of Canada's largest producing orchards, and it is only 10 minutes from the centre of Kelowna. It is also one if the oldest, having planted its first trees in 1905. KLO offers guided tours during summer months so you can see firsthand how the fruit is grown and taste the apple cider or fresh-pressed apple juice made on-site. By pairing local apples from a farm such as KLO with quinoa, which is a seed from a plant in the same family as spinach and buckwheat, you can offer your guests an incredibly healthy and tasty salad. Quinoa is available in the grains section of large grocery stores and health food stores across BC.

juice from 1 lemon

⅓ cup (75 mL) apple cider vinegar

½ cup (125 mL) orange juice

⅓ cup (75 mL) canola or sunflower oil

⅓ cup (75 mL) honey

5 cups (1.25 L) cooked quinoa (see Tip)

2 apples, cored and chopped

1 bell pepper, diced small

1 cup (250 mL) fresh corn kernels

½ cup (125 mL) dried cranberries

½ cup (125 mL) currants

1 small red onion, finely chopped

1 cup (250 mL) toasted, chopped pecans

1 cup (250 mL) fresh parsley and mint, chopped

sea salt and freshly ground pepper to taste

Place lemon juice, apple cider vinegar, orange juice, oil and honey in a small bowl and stir to combine.

In a large bowl, combine quinoa, apples, bell pepper, corn, cranberries, currants, onion, pecans, herbs, salt and pepper, then stir in dressing. Adjust seasonings and refrigerate until ready to serve.

Tip

To cook quinoa, bring 4 cups (1 L) of water to a boil in a wide-bottomed pot with a lid. Add a pinch of salt and stir in 2 cups (500 mL) of quinoa. Reduce heat to a simmer, cover and cook until all the water has absorbed, about 25 minutes. You can cook any amount of quinoa you like as long as you keep the 2:1 ratio of liquid to grain. It is also worth experimenting with other liquids such as stock or coconut milk.

 *If there is any leftover quinoa, you can warm it up and add a little cinnamon and cream for a nice breakfast.*

Heirloom Tomato Salad

Serves 4

If you are interested in tomatoes—those tomatoes reminiscent of days in the garden as a child picking the sun-warmed fruit right off the vine—then look no further than Stoney Paradise Farm tomatoes and Milan Djordjevich. In past years Milan could be found at the Granville Island Farmers' Market. Be sure to call Stoney Paradise Farm to find out where he and his tomatoes will be this summer!

1 clove garlic, minced

splash of white balsamic vinegar

¼ cup (60 mL) olive oil

sea salt and freshly ground pepper to taste

1 lb (500 g) heirloom tomatoes, washed, cored and sliced ½ in (1.25 cm) thick

½ lb (250 g) bocconcini, sliced ½ in (12 mm) thick

handful of fresh basil leaves, washed and patted dry

crusty French baguette

Place garlic, vinegar and oil in a salad bowl. Add tomatoes, tossing gently to coat with dressing. Season to taste with salt and pepper.

On individual plates, layer tomato slices with bocconcini and some basil tucked in between and around tomato slices. Scatter remaining basil leaves on top and drizzle remaining dressing. Serve with slices of crusty French baguette.

Tip

Fresh tomatoes from the garden or the farmers' market would also work in this recipe.

Bocconcini is a semi-ripe mozzarella cheese that comes in small, soft, white balls.

Heirloom tomato seeds are used in developing new tomato varieties that have natural resistance to viral, fungal and bacterial diseases.

Fresh Pea and Mint Pasta Salad

Serves 4 to 6 as a side dish

Fresh peas are a hallmark of early summer in southwestern British Columbia and are a favourite crop among backyard gardeners and commercial growers alike. BC produces more than 9900 tons (9000 tonnes) of peas each year, 90% of which are shelled and processed; however, on the home front, fresh green peas that are shelled at the sink are more likely to be eaten on the spot than make it to the table! A cool-climate crop, peas come into season in June and are available fresh at local farmers' markets, U-pick farms, produce merchants and many grocery stores. BC produces the highest quality and highest yielding peas in all of North America.

1 x 12 oz (340 g) package pasta, cooked and cooled (see Tip)

1 cup (250 mL) cherry tomatoes, halved

½ small red onion, halved and very thinly sliced

2 cups (500 mL) fresh peas

2 Tbsp (30 mL) fresh mint, finely chopped

1 Tbsp (15 mL) fresh oregano, finely chopped

1 cup (250 mL) chopped roasted chicken (optional)

Dressing

2 Tbsp (30 mL) white wine vinegar

¼ cup (60 mL) olive oil

½ tsp (2 mL) Dijon mustard

3 Tbsp (45 mL) mayonnaise

sea salt and freshly ground pepper to taste

In a large bowl, gently toss pasta, tomatoes, onion, peas, mint, oregano and chicken.

In a small bowl, whisk all dressing ingredients together. Pour over salad and toss. Serve immediately or store, covered, in refrigerator until ready to serve.

Tip

Pasta such as gemelli, fusilli, rotini or radiatore are perfect for pasta salads because their texture holds the dressing nicely.

Peas are a legume and, like most legumes, have special nodules on their roots that enable them to take nitrogen from the air and return it to the soil. This function actually allows the peas to enrich the soil they grow in.

Sweet Corn Bisque

Serves 6

Summer days are long and hot in August, and for many BC families, they are the perfect time to hit the road and head to the Fraser Valley or up to the Shuswap. Summer is also corn season, and people year after year return to their favourite stands with claims that they have found the sweetest corn in the province. For those who are city-bound, fresh-picked corn is trucked in and appears at farmers' markets, where people will line up for a taste of summer. Although nothing is as good as corn eaten off the cob, this bisque is a refined way to enjoy the sweetness created by the summer sun.

8 cups (2 L) corn kernels, fresh from cob or frozen, *divided*

1 Tbsp (15 mL) + ¼ cup (60 mL) butter, *divided*

sea salt and freshly ground pepper to taste

2 cups (500 mL) chopped yellow onion

1 clove garlic, minced

3 stalks celery, diced

2 medium carrots, diced

2 sprigs fresh thyme, minced

6 cups (1.5 L) stock

1 cup (250 mL) heavy cream (32%)

Tabasco to taste

tarragon sprigs and thinly sliced red pepper for garnish

In a pot, sauté 2 cups (500 mL) corn in 1 Tbsp (15 mL) of butter until cooked, about 5 minutes. Season with salt and pepper and set aside.

In same pot, sauté onions in ¼ cup (60 mL) of butter until translucent. Add garlic, celery and carrots and sauté for 5 minutes. Add remaining 6 cups (1.5 L) corn and thyme. Cover with stock and simmer for 20 minutes. Purée in batches in a blender to make a smooth soup and return to heat. Stir in cream, and season with salt, pepper and Tabasco. Garnish each bowl with reserved corn, tarragon and red pepper. Serve hot.

Corn Bread

Preheat oven to 400° F (205° C). Sift together flour, baking powder and salt. Stir in cornmeal. In a separate bowl, cream butter and sugar together, then beat in eggs, one at a time. Stir in buttermilk, then lightly fold wet and dry mixtures together, being sure not to overmix. Bake in 2 buttered 1 lb (1 L) loaf pans for 30 to 35 minutes until tester comes out clean.

Corn Bread

2 cups (500 mL) flour

1 Tbsp (15 mL) baking powder

1 tsp (5 mL) sea salt

2 cups (500 mL) cornmeal

1¼ cups (310 mL) butter

⅓ cup (75 mL) sugar

3 eggs

2 cups (500 mL) buttermilk

Tuna Carpaccio

Serves 6 to 8

Albacore tuna caught in the waters off of British Columbia's west coast is available fresh from late June through early fall. Its increasing popularity on the fresh sheet at local fishmongers is largely a result of our love affair with Japanese sushi. BC's albacore is fished in a sustainable manner, which avoids possible bycatch problems and yields lower mercury levels, thus meeting the Vancouver Aquarium Ocean Wise program criteria honoured by many top restaurateurs. This recipe showcases albacore tuna's fresh, mild flavour and succulent texture. Be sure to use sashimi-grade fish from a reliable fishmonger.

1 x 3 to 4 lbs (1.5 to 2 kg) sashimi-quality tuna loin, skinned and trimmed of any sinew

¼ cup (60 mL) fresh thyme, very finely chopped

¼ cup (60 mL) fresh mint, very finely chopped

1 long green chili, such as jalepeño or serrano, seeded and finely chopped

grated zest and juice of 1 lime

1 Tbsp (15 mL) rice wine vinegar

¼ cup (60 mL) sesame oil

mesclun and lime wedges for garnish

Roll tuna loin in thyme and mint, ensuring it is completely coated. Wrap tightly in plastic wrap and refrigerate for 2 hours.

Combine chili, lime zest and juice, vinegar and sesame oil to make dressing. When ready to serve, unwrap tuna and cut into paper-thin slices with a very sharp knife. Drizzle dressing over slices of tuna on serving plates with mesclun and lime wedges on side.

Tip

It is easier to slice tuna into paper-thin slices when it is partially frozen. Thaw it slightly to coat with herbs and then refreeze before slicing.

Serrano peppers are small, cylindrical-shaped peppers that can be either green or red. Although too hot for the palates of many Canadians, the peppers are actually relatively low on the Scoville scale with a rating of 10,000 to 20,000 (compared to the Scotch bonnet's 80,000 to 300,000 rating).

Seafood Chowder

Serves 6

This recipe is an adaptation of the signature seafood soup created by Edible Canada's Chef de Cuisine, Jennifer Dodd. Unlike a traditional seafood soup, this gorgeous soup features flavours of Asia that pair beautifully with the West Coast seafood. At the restaurant, Chef Dodd takes advantage of the season's spot prawn harvest to create batches of a rich seafood stock using the roasted prawn shells and heads. For the purpose of replicating this dish at home, we have simplified it by using fish stock. Be sure to choose your seafood from sustainable sources.

Coconut Broth

3 Tbsp (45 mL) vegetable oil

2 onions, diced

3 cloves garlic, minced

1½ Tbsp (22 mL) ginger

4 tsp (20 mL) tomato paste

2 tsp (10 mL) Thai red curry paste

4 cups (1 L) coconut milk

2 cups (500 mL) fish stock

4 tsp (20 mL) brown sugar

2 tsp (10 mL) fish sauce

juice of 2 limes

sea salt and pepper to taste

(continued on next page)

In a large pot on medium heat, add oil and onions and cook until browned. Add garlic and ginger, then add tomato paste and curry paste. Reduce heat to low and cook, stirring, for about 5 minutes.

Add coconut milk and cook until mixture is reduced by half, then add stock. Simmer for 45 minutes. Remove from heat. Add brown sugar, fish sauce and lime juice and stir. Season with salt and pepper to taste.

For chowder, add half of oil to a large pan on medium heat. Pat scallops dry and season with sea salt. Sear scallops on one side for about 3 minutes until caramelized. Remove pan from heat and set aside (do not flip—the heat from pan will finish cooking scallops).

Add remaining oil to pan. Season sablefish and salmon with sea salt. Sear for about 3 minutes. Add shrimp, mussels, clams and seafood broth. Simmer until mussels and clams are all open; discard any that do not open. Taste and adjust seasoning if needed.

Divide soup among 6 bowls and garnish with seared scallops, carrot and daikon.

Chowder

⅓ cup (75 mL) vegetable oil, divided

12 Qualicum Bay scallops

sea salt to taste

5 oz (140 g) sablefish fillet, diced

5 oz (140 g) steelhead salmon fillet, diced

12 side-stripe shrimp, peeled

30 mussels, scrubbed and debearded

30 clams

18 strips of tricoloured carrot curls

¼ daikon, cut into curls

Kimchee Crab Cakes

Makes 30 cakes

It used to be a rite of passage for many youngsters to wade into the briny, seaweed-rich waters of the Pacific during the summer months in search of Dungeness crab to bring home and boil for dinner. Nowadays, this crab is much easier to find at a local merchant such as T & T Market (where you can also find the kimchee), the Lobster Man on Granville Island or even the infamous Crab Shop on Dollarton Highway. But one thing remains the same: the sweet-salty meat from a Dungeness crab is the best in the world and is almost perfect in its naked form. These crab cakes have just a few ingredients because we don't want to mask the flavour of this West Coast treasure!

1 lb (500 g) fresh
Dungeness crab meat,
cartilage removed,
squeezed dry

½ cup (125 mL) finely
chopped cabbage kimchee,
drained

3 Tbsp (45 mL) chopped
green onion

¼ tsp (1 mL) pepper

2 white bread slices,
torn into pieces

1 egg

2 Tbsp (30 mL) mirin

2 tsp (10 mL) Korean hot
pepper paste

2 Tbsp (30 mL) canola oil,
divided

Combine crab meat, kimchee, green onion and pepper in a medium bowl.

Process bread in a blender or food processor until it becomes fine crumbs and add to crab mixture.

Process egg, mirin and hop pepper paste until smooth. Add to bowl and mix well. Shape into patties, about 1 in (2.5 cm) in diameter, using about 1 Tbsp (15 mL) for each.

Heat 1 Tbsp (15 mL) oil in a large frying pan on medium. Cook crab cakes in 2 batches for 3 minutes per side until browned.

Made from fermented cabbage, kimchee is a fiery condiment that is a staple in Korean kitchens and provides a quick way to give an aromatic flare to your meal. Assorted varieties of vegetables may be used to create other types of kimchee.

Panko and Coconut Spot Prawns

Serves 6

Shrimp is one of the most popular seafoods in North American, but 90% of the shrimp we eat is imported, much of it coming from environmentally shady aquaculture farms in Southeast Asia. For a sustainable option closer to home, look for spot prawns. Spot prawns are named for the distinctive white spots that adorn their shells. Highly regarded for their size and firm, sweet flesh, spot prawns are the largest of the seven shrimp species caught commercially in BC's coastal waters; females are known to grow to 9 in (23 cm) in length or more. Spot prawns are usually sold fresh for just over 11 weeks beginning in May, mostly in BC, but they are available frozen year-round.

1 cup (250 mL) flour

sea salt and freshly ground pepper

3 eggs, beaten

1 cup (250 mL) panko (see Tip, p. 11)

½ cup (125 mL) shredded unsweetened coconut

24 spot prawns, shelled, deveined, tail on

4 cups (1 L) peanut oil, for frying

½ cup (125 mL) Thai chili dipping sauce

Place flour in a bowl or shallow baking dish and season with salt and pepper. Beat eggs in a separate bowl. Combine panko and coconut in another shallow dish. Dredge prawns first in flour, then in beaten eggs and finally coat in panko mixture. Carefully lay prawns out in a single layer on a baking sheet.

Pour oil into a heavy-bottomed skillet and heat to 360° F (180° C); if you do not have a thermometer, test oil with a cube of bread—it should turn golden in under 2 minutes.

Cook prawns in small batches until golden, about 2 minutes, then transfer to a plate lined with paper towel. Serve hot with dipping sauce.

Tip

Whenever possible, buy your prawns with heads on. Keeping them whole is worth the extra work and ensures the flavourful juices are retained in the flesh. Thaw frozen prawns in the refrigerator overnight and use immediately.

Cedar-Planked Salmon with Lemon-Pistachio Crust

Serves 4 to 6

Abundant year-round and easily harvested along spawning routes, salmon were traditionally key resources for West Coast First Nations. Equally abundant and important were the cedar trees on the coast. It made sense for the First Nations people to cook their freshly caught salmon on easily split cedar planks. They filleted the salmon and cooked it skin side down, secured to the plank with saplings. The plank was then propped at an angle above the fire, thus perfuming the meat with a delicate, smoky flavour. Home cooks can still use this traditional method of preparation today. Just remember, always use wild salmon and be sure to soak the cedar plank for at least two hours before cooking.

1 cup (250 mL) unsalted, shelled pistachios, chopped

⅔ cup (150 mL) panko (see, p. 11)

2 Tbsp (30 mL) olive oil

1 Tbsp (15 mL) fresh dill, chopped

2 tsp (10 mL) Dijon mustard

zest from 1 lemon

¼ cup (60 mL) lemon juice

4 to 6 x 8 oz (250 g) skin-on salmon fillets, any species

2 cedar planks (see Tip)

sea salt and pepper to taste

Preheat grill to medium-high. Mix pistachios and panko together—it works especially well to pulse them together in a food processor. Place on a plate and set aside.

Mix oil, dill, mustard, zest and lemon juice to form a paste. Spread paste evenly on flesh side of each salmon fillet, then dip in pistachio and panko mixture. As they are crusted, lay fillets skin side down on prepared planks. Season crust with sea salt and freshly ground pepper. Place planks on grill, close lid and cook 12 to 15 minutes.

Tip

Purchase untreated cedar planks, 1 in (2.5 cm) thick, 8 in (20 cm) wide and 12 in (30 cm) long, from your local lumberyard or gourmet shop or via the Internet. The planks must be soaked in water for a minimum of 2 hours, but 4 to 6 hours is best. Drain and pat dry; brush with oil before using. They can often be cleaned and reused several times.

Tip

If not available at your supermarket, get pre-shelled, unsalted pistachios at a Mediterranean or Middle Eastern food store.

Piquant Cream Dill Sauce

Combine all ingredients together in a bowl. Refrigerate sauce for several hours before you plan to serve salmon, so flavours can come together.

Experiment with the crust mixture for this recipe or for use with other fish, chicken or meats. A blend of fresh chopped herbs works especially well, or you can add dried, chopped fruit such as apricots or cranberries. For added crunchiness, substitute cornmeal for some of the breadcrumbs.

Piquant Cream Dill Sauce

1 cup (250 mL) sour cream

3 Tbsp (45 mL) mayonnaise

¼ cup (60 mL) fresh dill, finely chopped

1 to 2 Tbsp (15 to 30 mL) drained capers, finely chopped

1 jalapeño pepper, seeds and membrane removed, finely chopped

1 green onion, white and green parts, finely chopped

1 tsp (5 mL) fresh lemon juice

sea salt and freshly ground pepper to taste

Wild BC Sablefish and Lentils with Vinaigrette

Serves 4

Sablefish is one of the hottest items on many of BC's top restaurant menus. Sablefish, also known as black cod or butterfish, is caught in the deep waters far off the coast of BC. Traditionally, most sablefish has been exported to Japan and Hong Kong, but it is now commonly available at many fishmongers around the province. Whether you buy it smoked or fresh, its sweet flavour and large white flakes are always sure to please. This recipe uses fresh herbs to complement the rich, oily texture of fresh sablefish.

4 x 4 oz (125 g) sablefish

sea salt and freshly ground pepper

splash of olive oil

1 cup (250 mL) cooked red lentils (see Tip)

¼ cup (60 mL) olive oil

¼ cup (60 mL) lemon juice

1 Tbsp (15 mL) fresh thyme, chopped

1 Tbsp (15 mL) fresh chives, chopped

1 Tbsp (15 mL) orange zest

½ lb (250 g) mixed salad greens with fresh herbs

Season sablefish with salt and pepper. Heat a small pan over medium-high and add a splash of oil. Sear fish, about 2 to 3 minutes per side. Remove from heat and set aside.

Mix warmed, cooked lentils in a bowl with olive oil, lemon juice, thyme, chives, orange zest, salt and pepper. Serve grilled sablefish on a bed of lentils and mixed salad with fresh herbs.

Tip

To cook lentils, pour 1 cup (250 mL) of cleaned, dry lentils into 3 cups (750 mL) salted, boiling water. Reduce heat and simmer until the lentils are *al dente,* about 20 minutes. 1 cup (250 mL) of dry lentils makes 2 to 2½ cups (500 to 625 mL) of cooked lentils.

Lentils are practically folic acid pills: 1 cup provides 90% of the recommended daily allowance. There is more folic acid in lentils that in any other unfortified food.

Pacific Scallops with Double Smoked Bacon and Vanilla

Serves 4

Pacific scallops are always a treat (when you can get them), but when paired with double smoked bacon and a hint of vanilla, they are incredible. For this recipe, try to get your hands on some bacon from Oyama Sausage. With more than 90% of its products made using locally raised BC pork, Oyama makes some of the finest tasting bacon you will find. And since Oyama has more than a dozen varieties, you can choose from many other kinds if double smoked bacon is not your preference. Oyama prides itself on producing the highest quality products and ensures that its pigs are raised using only the finest feed, including organic hazelnuts, to ensure the best possible flavour in the meat.

⅔ cup (150 mL) diced double smoked bacon

2 Tbsp (30 mL) minced shallots

1 cup (250 mL) dry BC sparkling wine

½ vanilla bean pod

½ tsp (2 mL) champagne vinegar, plus extra for dressing

1 cup (250 mL) cold unsalted butter, cut into small pieces

sea salt and freshly ground white pepper to taste

12 Pacific scallops

1 Tbsp (15 mL) olive oil, plus extra for dressing

1 bunch watercress, tough stems removed, cleaned and spun dry

fresh chives

In a medium saucepan, sauté bacon until crispy. Set bacon aside and stir in shallots, sparkling wine, vanilla bean pod and seeds (see Tip), and bring to a boil. Reduce heat to medium-low and simmer until you have about 1/4 cup (60 mL) of liquid remaining. Stir in champagne vinegar and remove vanilla pod. Turn heat down to very low and, little by little, whisk in butter, 1 piece at a time. Continue until all butter pieces have been added and sauce will coat back of a spoon. Stir in bacon, and season sauce with salt and pepper. Keep sauce warm but off direct heat until ready to serve.

Season scallops on all sides with salt and pepper. Place olive oil in a large pan over medium-high heat. When oil is hot, add scallops and sear for 2 to 3 minutes until nicely caramelized. Turn scallops over and cook for an additional 3 minutes.

For dressing, toss watercress in a bowl with a splash of olive oil and champagne vinegar, and season with salt and pepper. Serve scallops immediately with sauce, watercress and chives.

Tip

To get the most flavour out of a vanilla bean pod, carefully slice it open and scrape out the tiny seeds; use both seeds and pod in the recipe.

A vanilla bean can be used to infuse sugar with its wonderful aroma and flavour. Cut a vanilla bean in half lengthwise (or dry and reuse the pod from the recipe) and cover with 1 to 2 cups (250 to 500 mL) of white sugar for 3 to 4 weeks or more, stirring once a week. You can use vanilla sugar in your coffee or tea, or add it to whipped cream.

Grilled Beef Tenderloin with Sautéed Chanterelles

Serves 4

Most British Columbians associate quality Canadian beef with our neighbours to the east, where Alberta has reigned supreme in the cattle industry for decades. However, the Blue Goose Cattle Company in the southern Cariboo is trying to change that. On more than 250,000 acres (101,000 hectares) of land, Blue Goose raises both premium and organic beef that is finding its way onto restaurant menus and into high-end butcher shops around the province. What sets this high-quality, pasture-raised beef apart from others is the taste, and meat lovers will find that Blue Goose is worth the premium price.

Mushrooms

1 to 2 Tbsp (15 to 30 mL) olive oil

3 shallots, sliced

1 lb (500 g) fresh chanterelles

1 clove garlic, minced

½ cup (125 mL) white wine

1 cup (250 mL) parsley, chopped

¼ cup (60 mL) chives, chopped

sea salt and freshly ground black pepper

4 x 6 oz (170 g) beef tenderloin medallions

olive oil, for brushing

2 tsp (10 mL) kosher salt

freshly ground black pepper

Remove beef medallions from refrigerator 15 minutes before cooking.

To prepare mushrooms, heat olive oil in a skillet over medium-high and sauté shallots until soft. Add chanterelles and garlic and continue to sauté for 5 to 7 minutes, then add white wine and cook until liquid evaporates. Remove from heat and stir in parsley and chives. Season with salt and pepper. Set aside.

Heat grill or a stove-top grill pan to medium high. Brush beef lightly with olive oil and season with salt and pepper. Place on grill and cook, without moving, until nice grill marks appear, about 4 minutes. Turn medallions and continue to grill until medium-rare, about 3 to 4 minutes more. Set aside on a cutting board to rest for 5 minutes before serving.

Divide medallions among plates and spoon on mushrooms.

Shallots are related to onions and have a similar, but milder, flavour. In their appearance, however, they more closely resemble garlic. Shallots grow bulbs with multiple cloves, each separated by a papery skin. Fresh green shallots can be purchased seasonally, but dry shallots are more commonly available.

Beef Burgers

Serves 4

The hamburger originated in Hamburg, Germany—sort of. There was no bun, no ketchup and no drive-through; it was just a ground-meat patty known as "Hamburg Steak." Over the years, several Americans have claimed credit for inventing the burger as we know it, leading at times to heated controversy. It is generally agreed that the burger first reached national exposure during the St. Louis World's Fair in 1904. Hamburgers form the backbone of the fast-food industry, but that doesn't mean they are inherently unhealthy. Grass-fed beef is high in healthful omega-3 fatty acids and conjugated linoleic acid (CLA), an antioxidant and potentially healthful fat.

1½ lbs (680 g) ground beef

1 large egg

1 Tbsp (15 mL) grainy Dijon mustard

1 Tbsp (15 mL) chopped dill pickle

⅓ cup (75 mL) Parmesan cheese

freshly ground pepper

Preheat grill to high. Mix all ingredients together and form into 4 thick patties; thick patties make juicy burgers.

Grill patties, turning once, for 4 to 6 minutes per side, until internal temperature reaches 160° F (70° C). Serve patties on toasted buns with your favourite accompaniments including ketchup, mustard, sautéed onions and mushrooms, lettuce, tomato and anything else you desire.

Tip

For a better burger...

- Only use medium ground beef for burgers as lean or extra lean do not offer enough fat to create that great flavor and texture. Ask your local butcher to fresh grind chuck for you for a true gourmet burger.

- Handling the meat lightly when mixing and shaping will help prevent it from turning into a hockey puck.

- Make sure the grill is hot to seal in the juices and keep the meat from sticking.

- When shaping your patties, sneak an extra piece of your favourite cheese (e.g., Blue, Brie or Cheddar) in the centre, making sure it is completely surrounded by the meat, for a volcanic cheeseburger.

Here are some food safety tips when handling raw meat:

- *Store it in the refrigerator and use it within 2 days, or freeze it.*

- *Wash your hands and everything the meat contacted with a solution of 1 tsp (5 mL) unscented bleach per litre of water.*

- *Do not place the cooked burgers on the same surface the raw meat was on.*

- *Cook ground meat until it reaches 160° F (71° C) in temperature. E. coli is of particular concern for children, the elderly or anyone with a compromised immune system.*

Pemberton Potato Salad

Serves 4 to 6

The Pemberton Valley, north of Whistler, is home to rich agricultural lands that have become world famous for their seed potatoes as well as other root crops. In the late 1960s, the Pemberton Valley actually became the first farming community in the world to successfully grow virus-free seed potatoes. Today, many of the local farms, such as North Arm Farm owned by ski-patroller-turned-farmer-turned-mayor Jordon Sturdy, grow crops including corn, berries, flowers, squash and more. For this recipe, try to use Pemberton fingerling potatoes for their rich and buttery texture.

2 lbs (1 kg) potatoes, scrubbed

sea salt

2 carrots, diced

2 celery stalks, diced

1 x 8 oz (250 g) jar artichoke hearts, well drained and rinsed, then drained again and cut into eighths

1 green onion, white part only, finely chopped

1 red pepper, diced into small pieces

6 black olives, pitted and cut into slivers

6 baby gherkins, thinly sliced

¼ cup (60 mL) parsley, finely chopped

1 Tbsp (15 mL) capers, drained and chopped

¼ tsp (1 mL) sea salt

freshly ground black pepper

mayonnaise

Cook potatoes in gently boiling salted water until just tender. Once cooled, peel potatoes, cut into smallish cubes and set aside in a bowl. Meanwhile, cook carrots in gently boiling salted water for 5 minutes, then drain and refresh with cold water. Dry on a paper towel. Combine carrots and remaining ingredients with potatoes and mix in enough mayonnaise for a nice creamy texture. Serve immediately or chill until ready to serve.

Capers are actually the flower buds from a shrub native to the Mediterranean and parts of Asia. Once these buds are picked, they are sun-dried and then pickled in brine. Capers should always be rinsed and drained prior to use to remove any excess salt.

Minted Coleslaw

Serves 8

Often regarded as a health food, cabbage has been cultivated since before recorded history—although at first it was merely a few leaves and no head. Pythagoras recommended cabbage for longevity, and he lived to be over 80. The word coleslaw comes from the medieval Dutch *kool sla*, meaning "cabbage salad." Today, coleslaw graces nearly every picnic and barbecue in the land. Mint elevates this recipe from the mainstream into something memorable. At farmers' markets you can find great big green bunches of mint for a buck or two; an incredible bargain considering supermarket mint (when you can find it) is often $3 to $4 for a few wilted stems.

2 Tbsp (30 mL) grainy Dijon mustard

2 Tbsp (30 mL) sour cream

1 Tbsp (15 mL) mayonnaise

1 Tbsp (15 mL) olive oil

2 Tbsp (30 mL) apple cider vinegar

1 head of Savoy cabbage, shredded

1 small head of red cabbage, shredded (about 2 cups [500 mL])

1 fennel bulb, shredded

1 carrot, grated

6 radishes, grated

½ cup (125 mL) sliced green onion

½ cup (125 mL) thinly sliced fresh mint

Whisk together mustard, sour cream, mayonnaise, oil and vinegar for dressing. Combine both types of cabbage, fennel, carrot, radish, onion and mint together in a large bowl and add dressing. Toss well and let marinate at least 30 minutes before serving.

Tip

You can easily turn this recipe into an Asian slaw by omitting sour cream, mayonnaise, olive oil and mint and substituting 1 Tbsp (15 mL) of toasted sesame oil, 1 Tbsp (15 mL) of soy sauce, ½ cup (125 mL) of chopped of cilantro and a handful of toasted sesame seeds. Grilled and sliced turkey or chicken breast also makes a nice addition.

Char-grilled Corn with Jalapeño Lime Butter

Serves 6

Many of BC's warmest regions, including the Okanagan Valley and eastern Fraser Valley, produce the province's sweetest corn because of the combination of hot summer days and cooler nights—optimal conditions for increasing the sugar content. In BC, we produce more than 40 million pounds (18 million kilograms) of corn each year, but only a quarter of it goes unprocessed. Sadly, in our quest for sweet corn, we have lost many of the hundreds of varieties that were once common. This recipe combines one of summer's greatest treasures with a Mexican inspired butter that will have you heating up the barbecue all summer long!

6 ears of corn

Jalapeño Lime Butter

1 cup (250 mL) unsalted butter, softened

1 jalapeño pepper, seeded and finely chopped

zest from 1 lime

1 clove garlic, minced

1 tsp (5 mL) sea salt

lime wedges

sea salt to taste

Preheat barbecue to medium-high. Peel back husks, leaving them attached, and remove silk from corn. Rewrap, tying with butcher twine or kitchen string if necessary. Barbecue for about 10 minutes, turning to cook all sides. If husks start to burn, spritz them with water.

For jalapeño lime butter, mix ingredients together in a bowl or in a food processor. Wrap in plastic and shape into a cylinder about 1 in (2.5 cm) in diameter, and refrigerate.

Serve hot corn with rounds of jalapeño lime butter, lime wedges and sea salt.

Tip

To keep the sugars from turning to starch, keep freshly picked corn as cool as possible and enjoy it soon after harvesting. Fresh corn can be steamed, boiled or grilled, and older corn can be cut from the cob and added to soups and stews.

 *Sweet corn, which is the corn that we eat fresh, is the result of a gene mutation in field corn. This mutation occurred in the 1800s in the United States and prevented sugar in the kernel from being converted to starch.*

Barbecued BC Peaches with Camembert

Serves 6

Juicy and sweet, British Columbian peaches are at their best in mid-July. A road trip through BC's southern Okanagan region, Canada's most important peach-growing area, is incomplete without a stop at one of the many fruit stands that line the roads of the Similkameen Valley. Just one bite into the yellow or white flesh is truly a taste of summer in BC. To experience the best of BC's peaches, be sure to head out to the Penticton Peach Festival, held every year in early to mid-August. The festival originated in 1947 and is now a five-day extravaganza filled with parades, live music and much more.

2 Tbsp (30 mL) canola or grape seed oil

1 Tbsp (15 mL) honey

pinch of sea salt

pinch of pepper

6 peaches, pitted and sliced in half

4 oz (125 g) Camembert, cut into 6 wedges

6 fresh basil leaves

Preheat barbecue to medium-high. Combine oil, honey, salt and pepper in a bowl. Brush peaches with glaze and grill flesh side down for 3 minutes. Place peaches flesh side up on a baking sheet and place a basil leaf and a wedge of Camembert on top of each peach. Return peaches on baking sheet to barbecue, close lid and cook until cheese is melted, about 5 minutes.

Peaches are the stone fruit from a tree that originated in China, where peaches are an important symbol for a long life and immortality.

Iced Tea with Fresh Mint

Serves 4

There are two traditional types of iced tea—sweetened and unsweetened. In BC, the general preference seems to be for the sweetened variety, with many variations possible because of our province's obsession with all things healthy and ethnic. Beyond the traditional black tea, you can make iced tea using roiboos tea from South Africa, green teas from China, chai from India or even matcha from Japan. Don't forget to add mint or a few slices of orange or lemon to improve the flavour even more. Granville Island Tea Company offers one of BC's best selections of fine quality teas along with the best prices.

6 cups (1.5 L) cold water

5 level tsp (25 mL) good quality, loose tea

⅔ cup (150 mL) white sugar, or to taste

handful of fresh mint, rinsed and patted dry

1 orange or lemon

Bring water to a boil. Place tea in a pitcher and pour boiling water over tea. Let infuse for 30 minutes.

Stir in sugar to dissolve and strain tea into a clean pitcher.

Bruise mint by crushing it lightly with a rolling pin or bottom of a glass, and place in pitcher.

Chill tea at least 1 hour. Remove mint and serve with wedge of lime or lemon and a sprig of mint, if desired.

Traditionally, iced tea was served as a refreshing punch spiked with alcohol. The version we think of most often today, a freshly brewed tea sweetened and flavoured with lemon, first became popular after being served at the 1904 St. Louis World's Fair

Some people call the alcohol-spiked version of iced tea "iced tea on a stick." Iced coffee is also a popular summer drink available homemade or purchased from fine coffee shops throughout the province.

Birchwood Dairy Yogurt and Honey Semifreddo

Serves 4 to 6

This recipe draws inspiration from the numerous ice cream and gelato shops that service just about every neighbourhood in Vancouver. Semifreddo is easier to make than ice cream, and it is as delicious as the homemade gelato available around the corner. But where to get BC yogurt? Birchwood Dairy is a family-owned farm in the Fraser Valley that produces fine dairy products, including yogurt. A perfect combination of slightly tart and super creamy, this is the yogurt of choice to blend with any premium BC honey, and it will keep your guests coming back for more!

2¼ cups (560 mL) heavy cream (32%)

5 egg yolks 1/2 cup (125 mL) honey 1/2 cup (125 mL) unflavoured yogurt

In a mixer, whisk cream to stiff peaks. Transfer whipped cream into another bowl and set aside. Clean and dry mixing bowl and whisk yolks with honey until pale yellow and thickened. Fold in yogurt. Then fold in whipped cream.

Line a mould with plastic wrap. Place filling into mould. Cover and freeze for 24 hours. Remove semifreddo from freezer just before serving. Top with your favourite berries.

Bee-keeping in BC is a huge industry, not for the sweet honey that the bees produce, but rather for the pollination of flowering crops. In fact, the value of bees to agriculture is worth 10 to 20 times the value of all honey and bee products combined. Bees are crucial to BC's cranberry production, for example, and are "employed" during the spring to pollinate the crops.

Semifreddo *is Italian for "half-cold" and describes the half-frozen or chilled nature of this delicious confection.*

Ruth's Unbaked Strawberry Cheesecake

Serves 8

The first strawberries of the season are generally ready for harvest sometime in June and are one of the first fruits each season that signify the start of summer. In BC, we grow over 6 million pounds (2.7 million kilograms) of strawberries a year, which is more than a quarter of Canada's total production. The bulk of these come from the Fraser Valley, where many U-pick farms feature strawberries and attract a loyal following each year. For the do-it-yourself type of person, strawberries are easy to grow in a container garden on your deck or balcony. This recipe is an unbaked cheesecake, which we find creamier and not as heavy as baked cheesecakes, and it's more suited to the juicy strawberries.

Crust

2 cups (500 mL) graham wafer crumbs

½ cup (125 mL) + 1 Tbsp (15 mL) unsalted butter, melted

zest of 1 lemon, finely chopped

Filling

3 x 8 oz (250 g) packages cream cheese, at room temperature

½ to 1 cup (125 to 250 mL) icing sugar, sifted

fresh lemon juice

⅓ cup (75 mL) whipping cream (32%)

Topping

1 x 8 oz (250 mL) jar of apple jelly

1 lb (500 g) strawberries, whole, washed and stemmed

For crust, preheat oven to 350° F (175° C). In a mixing bowl, combine graham wafer crumbs, melted butter and lemon zest. Pat mixture evenly into a 10 in (25 cm) pie plate (see Tip). Bake in preheated oven for 10 minutes. Cool to room temperature. Cover and chill in refrigerator until ready to fill. Crust can be made a day in advance.

For filling, combine cream cheese, icing sugar and a generous squeeze of lemon juice in a food processor. Mix until smooth and creamy. Transfer to a large mixing bowl.

In a small bowl, beat whipping cream until light and fluffy, and fold into cream cheese mixture. Gently fill chilled graham crust with creamy filling and chill for at least 3 hours before serving.

For topping, gently heat apple jelly until just warm in a small saucepan. In a medium bowl, pour warm jelly over strawberries and mix lightly. Arrange glazed strawberries on top of cheesecake.

Tip

You can use the bottom of a small glass to help press the graham wafer crumbs evenly on the pie plate.

The name "strawberry" is derived from the Old English streawberige, with streaw meaning "straw" and berige meaning "berry." In parts of northern Europe, wild berries are still commonly gathered by threading them onto a straw, giving a possible origin for the name.

Cherry Pie

Serves 6 to 8

Nothing is more BC than cherry pie in summer. The province's farmers produce more than 12 million pounds (5.5 million kilograms) of sweet cherries and 2.2 million pounds (1 million kilograms) of sour cherries each year, with varieties such as Bing, Lambert, Van, Lapins, Stella and Sweethearts. With the proliferation of BC's wine industry, many cherries are being turned into fabulous fruit wines such as Elephant Island's Stella Cherry and Forbidden Fruit's Cerise d'Eve. If you can find these treasures, they will add a great splash of flavour to this pie or serve as the perfect accompaniment to some great dark chocolate.

Great Pie Crust

2½ cups (625 mL) flour

1 tsp (5 mL) sea salt

1 Tbsp (15 mL) sugar

1 cup (250 mL) unsalted butter, frozen

1 Tbsp (15 mL) lemon juice

about ⅓ cup (75 mL) ice water

Filling

6 cups (1.5 L) fresh pitted cherries

¾ cup (175 mL) sugar

juice from 1 lemon

2 Tbsp (30 mL) cornstarch

For crust, mix flour, salt and sugar in a bowl. Using a cheese grater, grate frozen butter into flour mixture. Toss lightly to distribute butter. Add lemon juice and enough water for dough just to come together. Divide in half, wrap each piece in plastic wrap and flatten into a disc. Chill for at least 30 minutes before using. Makes enough for a double-crusted pie.

For filling, preheat oven to 400° F (205° C). In a medium saucepan, mix cherries and sugar and cook over medium-low heat until most juice from cherries has reduced, about 15 minutes. Stir lemon juice and cornstarch together in a small bowl and add to cherries Cook, stirring until thick, about 7 minutes. Remove from heat and let cool to room temperature.

Pour cherry filling into prepared pastry crust and bake for 10 minutes. Reduce heat to 375° F (190° C) and bake for 20 to 30 minutes or until pastry is golden brown. Let cool before serving.

Tip

To make a lattice top, roll out and cut the remaining piece of dough into 1 in (2.5 cm) strips. Interlock the strips in a criss-cross weave over the pie filling and press the strips onto the edges of the bottom crust. Brush the pastry lightly with a glaze made with 1 beaten egg and 2 Tbsp (30 mL) milk.

Raspberry Tart

Serves 6 to 8

Fragrantly sweet and subtly tart, raspberries (*Rubus* spp.) are a favourite BC fruit. A member of the rose family, raspberries grow in almost all parts of the province, but more than 80% are produced in the Abbotsford area of the Fraser Valley. A fantastic crop of wild raspberries grows in central BC each year. An enterprising young man named Ryan Veitch has formed a company called Wild Berry Wholesome Foods, whose delectable line of jams and jellies feature only hand-picked wild fruits from around the province.

Crust

1¼ cups (310 mL) all-purpose flour

¼ cup (60 mL) sugar

½ cup (125 mL) or 1 stick unsalted butter, cold and cut into pieces

2 to 3 Tbsp (30 to 45 mL) cold water

Filling

2 x 8 oz containers (250 g) mascarpone, room temperature

½ cup (125 mL) sugar

1 tsp (5 mL) vanilla

3 cups (750 mL) raspberries

Glaze

1 x 8 oz (250 mL) jar of apple jelly

For crust, place flour, sugar and butter in a food processor and blend until mixture resembles coarse meal. Add 2 Tbsp (30 mL) of water until incorporated. Add enough remaining water, if necessary, until mixture comes together but is still crumbly. Wrap dough in plastic and refrigerate for 1 hour.

Preheat oven to 350° F (175° C). Press crust mixture evenly onto bottom and sides of an 11 in (28 cm) tart pan with removable fluted rim or 6 to 8 individual tart tins. Prick crust with a fork, line it with parchment and weigh it down with pie weights or dried beans. Bake in middle of oven until golden, about 15 minutes. Let cool to room temperature and chill for 1 hour in refrigerator.

Make filling while crust chills. In a medium bowl, using an electric mixer, beat mascarpone, sugar and vanilla together until smooth. Pour filling into chilled crust, spreading evenly, and arrange raspberries on top.

If keeping tart longer than a day, brush raspberries lightly with a glaze of warmed apple jelly.

Tip

When out picking raspberries in your yard or favourite U-pick farm, be sure to keep them as cool as possible, and store them unwashed. Ideally, pick them during cooler times of the day or on a cloudy day.

℘ *Mascarpone is a rich cream cheese that has the consistency of a stiff whipped cream. Originally produced in the Lombardy region of Italy, it is now available in grocery stores and Italian markets.*

℘ *Raspberries are healthy, antioxidant-rich berries high in ellagic acid—the same family of tannins that make wine, green tea and fruit such as pomegranates an important part of a healthy lifestyle.*

Tomato Salad with Bocconcini Tempura

Serves 4

In the Cowichan Valley, just outside the community of Duncan on Vancouver Island, is Fairburn Farm, home to Canada's only herd of water buffalo. The animals, born in BC, are the descendents of a herd of Bulgarian Murrah water buffalo imported from Denmark in 2000. Property owners Darrel and Anthea Archer have started milking their herd, and they sell the milk to Natural Pastures Cheese Company in Courtenay, and *they* create Canada's first traditional buffalo mozzarella—perfect for this recipe. You just have to make the trip to the Island to get it!

peanut oil

1 lb (500 g) assorted heirloom tomatoes, sliced into thick rounds

handful of fresh basil

17 oz (500 mL) container mini bocconcini, drained and patted very dry

1 recipe of tempura batter (see p. 142)

extra virgin olive oil or cold-pressed canola oil

juice of 1 lemon

sea salt and freshly ground pepper

Heat peanut oil in a pot or deep fryer to 375° F (190° C). Arrange sliced tomato and basil onto individual plates. Dip bocconcini into tempura batter and fry until golden. Serve tempura bocconcini together with tomato slices. Drizzle with oil and lemon juice. Season with salt and pepper.

Tip

For deep-frying, peanut oil should be 2 to 3 in (5 to 7.5 cm) deep in the pot, or use a deep fryer according to the manufacturer's directions.

Roasted Vancouver Figs

Serves 8

Dried figs are available in grocery stores throughout the province year-round, but why settle for dried when you can have fresh! Although they are native to the Mediterranean and southwest Asia, fig trees are quite at home in the Lower Mainland; large specimens laden with fruit can be found scattered throughout Vancouver in summer. Figs are delicate and typically do not fare well on long journeys, so before you buy imported figs from the supermarket, check your local farmers' market for fresh local product. You won't be disappointed!

8 slices Oyama speck or pancetta

8 large Vancouver-grown green fresh figs, cut in half

$\frac{1}{2}$ cup (125 mL) crumbled fresh goat cheese

1 Tbsp (15 mL) freshly cracked black pepper

drizzle of Whistler Balsamic Reduction (or balsamic reduction of your choice)

Preheat broiler to high. Heat a medium frying pan on medium. Fry speck until crisp and crumbly and set aside.

Place figs cut side up on a baking sheet. Sprinkle goat cheese and pepper on figs. Roast under broiler on second rack down for 3 to 5 minutes until figs have softened and cheese is starting to caramelize.

Top with crispy speck, drizzle with balsamic reduction and serve.

Dungeness Crab and Coconut Soup

Serves 4 to 6

Come fall, the days are still warm but evening comes sooner and a chill can be felt at night. Summer may be over, but local foods are just as bountiful as ever. Local Dungeness crab, available year-round, is best through August. The price of corn beckons buyers with screaming deals of six ears for a few bucks. At local farmers' markets, bulbous pale green fennel bulbs, sometimes with their feathery tops, sometimes without, are displayed next to the season's last bunches of basil. This soup celebrates fall in BC with light, yet warming flavours.

4 cups (1 L) chicken stock

2 cups (500 mL) fresh corn kernels cut from the cob, with cobs reserved (about 3 to 4 ears)

2 Tbsp (30 mL) olive oil

2 cups (500 mL) thinly sliced yellow onion

1 tsp (5 mL) toasted fennel seeds

1 fresh red chili, seeded and cut into slivers

1/2 tbsp (7 mL) cornstarch

2 1/2 cups (625 mL) coconut milk

juice and zest from 1 lime

1 lb (500 g) Dungeness crabmeat, cleaned

1 cup (250 mL) thinly sliced fresh fennel bulb

coarse sea salt and freshly ground pepper to taste

1/4 cup (60 mL) chopped cilantro leaves

1/4 cup (60 mL) chopped fresh basil

In a large saucepan, heat chicken stock to a low simmer. Add corn cobs, cover and simmer for 10 to 15 minutes.

Meanwhile, in a second large saucepan, heat olive oil over medium. Add onion, fennel seeds and chili. Sauté until softened, about 5 minutes.

Strain chicken stock and add to vegetable mixture; discard cobs. Dissolve cornstarch in coconut milk and add to broth, along with lime zest. Bring to a simmer and cook for 5 minutes. Add corn kernels, crab and fennel, and cook until warmed through, about 3 to 5 minutes. Add lime juice. Taste and adjust seasoning. Stir in cilantro and basil just before serving.

Coconut milk is coveted for its ability to mellow fiery flavours and add richness to curries and soups. It is made by combining equal parts of coconut meat and water, and simmering the mixture until it is foamy. The coconut meat is then strained out and discarded, leaving behind the milky liquid.

Spiced Parsnip and Cauliflower Soup

Serves 4 to 6

With its elegant ivory colour and sweet, complex flavour, the parsnip *(Pastinaca sativa)* is the queen of root vegetables. It can be used in everything from soups to main courses, and when combined with some melted butter and brown sugar, honey or birch syrup for a side dish, it tastes just like candy. The parsnip came to North America from Europe in the 17th century; this root crop is especially well suited to a short growing season in a cool climate in areas of BC like Pemberton and the Fraser Valley. The parsnip is best eaten late in fall, once it has benefited from exposure to frost.

2 to 3 Tbsp (30 to 45 mL) olive oil

1 Tbsp (15 mL) yellow mustard seeds

2 onions, finely chopped

2 cloves garlic, minced

1 tsp (5 mL) fresh ginger, finely chopped

1 Tbsp (15 mL) turmeric

1 tsp (5 mL) cardamom

1 tsp (5 mL) cumin

1 lb (500 g) cauliflower, trimmed and cut into florets

1 lb (500 g) parsnips, peeled and cut into chunks roughly the same size as the cauliflower

2 cups (500 mL) vegetable or chicken stock or water

1⅔ cups (400 mL) coconut milk

sea salt and freshly ground pepper to taste

1 Tbsp (15 mL) fresh cilantro, finely chopped

Heat oil in a large saucepan over medium-high. When oil is hot, add mustard seeds and cook until they begin to pop. Add onion, garlic and ginger, and cook for a couple of minutes until onion is soft and translucent. Add turmeric, cardamom and cumin. Add cauliflower and parsnip and cook, stirring, for a couple of minutes. Add stock or water to pan and bring it slowly to a boil. Skim off any scum that rises to top and reduce soup to a simmer. Leave it to cook gently for 30 minutes, stirring regularly.

Soup is ready when cauliflower is cooked and tender. Stir in coconut milk. Purée soup in blender until smooth and return to a clean saucepan. Season soup with salt and pepper, garnish with cilantro and serve.

Tip
Parsnips are best stored in a very cold location or in the refrigerator.

For a different snack, try making parsnip chips! Peel 3 or 4 parsnips lengthwise with a sharp vegetable peeler into long paper-thin strips until you've reached the central core. Heat oil in a medium-sized saucepan to 350° F (175° C) and drop parsnip strips in small batches and fry for 1 minute until crisp and golden. Drain on paper towels, season with sea salt and serve.

Pumpkin Fondue

Serves 12 as an appetizer

Just about everyone who got married during the 1970s received at least one fondue pot for a wedding present. Over three decades later, fondues have come back as a tasty, special part of a social gathering. They can be savoury or sweet, and there are many variations of the traditional cheese fondue. For example, an oil or broth can be used for meat fondues, and chocolate fondue is another popular version usually using fruit or cake for dipping. The following pumpkin fondue is a departure from the traditional, but it will have your guests talking!

1 x 3 to 4 lb (1.5 to 2 kg) sugar pumpkin

2 Tbsp (30 mL) unsalted butter

1 small onion, finely chopped

1 clove garlic, minced

1 cup (250 mL) dry white wine

pinch of freshly grated nutmeg

2 Tbsp (30 mL) flour

¼ cup (60 mL) fresh sage, chopped

2 cups (500 mL) grated aged white cheddar cheese

½ cup (125 mL) sour cream

sea salt and freshly ground pepper to taste

crusty bread

Preheat oven to 350° F (175° C). Pierce top of pumpkin with a knife 3 or 4 times, and bake for 20 minutes. Let cool for 10 minutes. Remove top quarter, forming a lid. Scoop out seeds and fibres and set aside. Increase oven temperature to 375° F (190° C).

Melt butter in a medium saucepan and sauté onion for 5 minutes. Add garlic and cook until softened. Add white wine and bring to a simmer. Finally, add nutmeg, flour, sage and cheddar cheese and stir until cheese is melted. Pour into pumpkin, cover with its lid and bake for 20 minutes until the mixture is hot. Remove from oven and stir in sour cream. Season with salt and pepper, and serve with skewers of crusty bread for dipping and spoons for scooping out the delicious pumpkin flesh.

The word "fondue" comes from the French verb *fondre*, "to melt." Originating in the Swiss Alps, fondue was born of necessity during the cold months when food was scarce. By melting hard, dry cheeses in a caquelon (a traditional, small earthenware pot) and enriching them with ingredients such as wine, a resourceful cook could transform even the stalest crust of bread into a delicious meal.

Coq au Vin with Okanagan Pinot Noir

Serves 6

British Columbia wines are earning an excellent reputation for quality within Canada and abroad. The Okanagan Valley lies at the same latitude as northern French and German vineyards. The northern Okanagan is producing some world-class, Alsatian-style whites, while the sandy desert soils of the south are ideal for varietals such as Pinot Gris, Chardonnay, Merlot, Cabernet Sauvignon and Pinot Noir. While many people think of Coq au Vin as a dish using red wine, it is actually meant to be a dish using the "local" wine, so many regions of France have variations of the dish—even Coq au Champagne! In this version we used Thomas Reid Chicken from the Fraser Valley and an Okanagan Pinot Noir, but the choice is up to you!

¼ cup (60 mL) + 2 Tbsp (30 mL) unsalted butter, *divided*

⅔ cup (150 mL) bacon, diced

1 x 3 to 4 lb (1.5 to 2 kg) free-range chicken, cut into 8 pieces

salt and freshly ground pepper

2 medium onions, chopped

1 carrot, chopped

1 cup (250 mL) celery root, diced

2 cloves garlic, sliced

2 Tbsp (30 mL) flour

1 bottle (750 mL) Okanagan Pinot Noir

4 sprigs of fresh thyme

8 cups (2 L) chicken stock

2 cups (500 mL) small white button mushrooms, left whole

Melt 2 Tbsp (30 mL) of butter in heavy-bottomed casserole and add bacon. Cook over medium heat until bacon is crisp. Drain on paper towels and place into a large bowl.

Season chicken pieces with salt and pepper and cook them in bacon drippings until golden brown. Transfer to bowl with bacon. Add onions, carrot and celery root to pan and cook slowly on medium heat, stirring from time to time, until onion is translucent. Add garlic, then stir in flour and let cook for 3 to 5 minutes. Add chicken, bacon, red wine, thyme and enough chicken stock to cover the chicken. Bring to a boil, reduce heat and cook, partially covered, for 45 minutes to 1 hour until the chicken is tender.

Meanwhile, melt remaining butter in a small pan and sauté mushrooms until golden. Season lightly with salt and pepper, then add to chicken. Ladle some sauce into a saucepan and reduce over high heat until thick and glossy. Serve chicken and sauce over hot buttered noodles.

∽ *This classic French dish, originally traced back to ancient Gaul and the times of Julius Caesar, is hearty and rich, with local chicken and fragrant herbs stewed in red wine. Age is definitely a virtue—in this recipe, using an older bird produces a richer flavour.*

Apple-roasted Pheasant

Serves 4

Apples and pheasant paired together make the perfect fall dish to celebrate a successful growing season. The flavours of the apple and herbs will penetrate the meat of the pheasant and lend an almost sweet taste to the bird. For extra flavour, you could also roast the pheasant on your barbecue and use some apple wood chips under the grate to add some smoky apple notes to the dish. This recipe can also be made with other poultry such as quail or chicken, and you could even experiment with other local fruits such as quince or pears.

4 pheasant breasts, skin on, wing attached

sea salt and freshly cracked black pepper

1 Tbsp (15 mL) butter

1 Tbsp (15 mL) grape seed or olive oil

4 cups (1 L) Pink Lady apples, peeled and sliced

¼ cup (60 mL) honey

1 Tbsp (15 mL) garlic, minced

1 tsp (5 mL) cinnamon

1 tsp (5 mL) cloves

juice of ½ lemon

Preheat oven to 425° F (220° C). Season pheasant with salt and pepper. Heat butter and oil in an ovenproof sauté pan that is large enough to comfortably fit meat. On medium-high heat, sear pheasant breasts, skin side down, for 3 to 4 minutes until golden brown. Set aside.

Combine apples, honey, garlic, cinnamon, cloves and lemon juice in a mixing bowl and sauté in same pan as pheasant. When apples are nicely caramelized, about 5 minutes, place pheasant on top, skin side up, and roast in oven for 10 to 12 minutes until meat is cooked through.

Serve breasts atop a spoonful of caramelized apples.

Native to Japan and China, the pheasant is a member of the Phasianidae family of birds, which includes the quail and the peacock. Terrestrial birds that can be distinguished by the male's ornate plumage, pheasants were introduced into North America in 1881.

Sweet and Sour Pork

Serves 6

Chinese immigrants started to settle in British Columbia in large numbers beginning with the Fraser River Gold Rush of 1858. In the early to mid-1880s, 17,000 Chinese men came to Canada to build the western section of the Canadian Pacific Railway. After the last spike was driven, these hard-working immigrants were left unemployed and received no assistance from the Canadian government. Using their strong cultural ties to food, many of these men opened restaurants, often along the route of the CPR. Today, Vancouver is home to one of North America's largest Chinatowns. Many of the region's Chinese restaurants are now reputed to be some of the best in the world!

2 Tbsp (30 mL) cornstarch

1 Tbsp (15 mL) cold water

1 lb (500 g) boneless pork loin rib, cut into bite-sized pieces

2 egg yolks

1 Tbsp (15 mL) soy sauce

2 tsp (10 mL) sea salt, *divided*

⅔ cup (150 mL) rice wine vinegar

¼ cup (60 mL) white wine

⅓ cup (75 mL) sugar

3 cloves garlic, minced

2 Tbsp (30 mL) grated fresh ginger

½ small pineapple, peeled, cored, quartered and sliced

1 small tomato, diced

½ cup (125 mL) julienned red pepper

1 tsp (5 mL) cinnamon

In a medium bowl, add cornstarch to water and mix well. Add pork, egg yolks, soy sauce and 1 tsp (5 mL) salt. Toss well, and refrigerate overnight.

Place vinegar, wine, sugar and remaining salt into a pan and bring to a boil. Add garlic and ginger; reduce heat and simmer for 10 minutes. Add pineapple, tomato, red pepper and cinnamon and simmer for an additional 10 minutes or until tomato becomes incorporated into sauce. Remove from heat and set sauce aside.

Heat oil to 350° F (175° C) to fry pork. Toss marinated pork in cornstarch and flour mixture and fry in hot oil until cooked, about 5 minutes. Drain well on kitchen towel. Heat sauce through, adding snow peas just before serving. Spoon sauce over pork and serve with rice or noodles.

(continued on next page)

Tip

Try this dish with other meats, such as chicken or beef; it also works well with tofu. The sauce can be made up to 3 days ahead and stored in the fridge.

vegetable oil for frying

¼ cup (60 mL) *each* cornstarch and flour, sifted together into a bowl

1 cup (250 mL) snow peas

Silky Chicken Curry

Serves 6

The first immigrants from India were Sikhs who landed in Vancouver in 1904; they found work mostly in the timber industry. Despite institutionalized discrimination that lasted well into the century, Sikhs and other Indians continued to arrive in BC and make their contribution to our multicultural landscape. Over the past decade, Indian cuisine has become a major player on the BC food scene. Indian restaurants have evolved from obscurity to the point where people will now wait over two hours for a table at one of the city's top Indian restaurants, Vij's. This popularity is attributable not only to the character and complexity of the cuisine, but to BC's huge ethnic population and love of unique cuisines.

¼ cup (60 mL) unsalted butter

3 medium onions, finely diced

3 cloves garlic, minced

1 Tbsp (15 mL) grated fresh ginger

⅓ cup (75 mL) curry paste

2 tsp (10 mL) freshly ground cumin

pinch of cayenne or chilies (optional)

2½ lbs (1.2 kg) diced chicken or a 4 lb (2 kg) chicken, cut into 10 pieces

2 medium carrots, peeled and diagonally sliced

1 red pepper, diced

1 medium tomato, diced

1 cup (250 mL) coconut milk

sea salt and freshly ground pepper

fresh cilantro, chopped

1 cup (250 mL) toasted and chopped unsalted cashews

Melt butter over medium heat in a wide, heavy-bottomed pot. Add onions, garlic and ginger and cook for about 5 minutes. Stir in curry paste, cumin and cayenne and cook for 2 minutes.

Add chicken, stirring to coat, then add carrots, red pepper, tomato and coconut milk. Bring to a simmer, cover and cook for about 30 minutes, or until chicken is cooked. Season with salt and pepper. Curry can be made up to 3 days in advance and refrigerated.

Serve curry hot, garnished with cilantro and cashews, accompanied by basmati or jasmine rice and a side of plain yogurt or raita (see opposite).

Tip

If you are afraid of cooking rice (and don't have an electric rice cooker), try this foolproof method. Cook your rice as you would cook pasta, in a big pot of boiling salted water. Check rice often for doneness, then drain in a fine mesh colander and serve. This method is especially suited to cooking large quantities of rice.

(continued on next page)

Peel, seed and grate cucumbers into a colander and let drain 15 minutes. Transfer grated cucumber to a bowl, squeezing out as much moisture as possible, then stir in yogurt, mint, cumin, salt and pepper. Store, refrigerated, for up to 5 days.

Raita

2 long English cucumbers

1 cup (250 mL) plain yogurt

¼ cup (60 mL) fresh chopped mint

ground cumin, sea salt and freshly ground pepper to taste

Cranberry Bison Meatballs

Serves 6 to 8

A cranberry glaze gives wonderful flavour to these bison meatballs—perfect to snack on in front of the big game and a great way to use up leftover cranberry sauce! For the BBQ sauce, choose one of the great local, award-winning sauces from Canadian BBQ champs such as Rock'in Ron Shewchuk or the House of Q's Brian Misko.

1 egg, fork-beaten

¼ cup (60 mL) sun dried cranberries

2 Tbsp (30 mL) olive oil

½ tsp (2 mL) ground allspice

½ tsp (2 mL) salt

¼ tsp (1 mL) pepper, divided

1 lb (500 g) medium ground bison

1 cup (250 mL) canned whole cranberry sauce

¼ cup (60 mL) barbecue sauce

1 tsp (5 mL) white vinegar

Combine egg, cranberries, oil, allspice, salt and ¼ tsp (0.5 mL) pepper in a large bowl.

Add bison and mix well. Roll into ¾ in (2 cm) balls. Arrange in single layer on greased baking sheet with sides. Cook in 375° F (190° C) oven for about 15 minutes until no longer pink inside.

For glaze, combine cranberry sauce, barbecue sauce, vinegar and remaining pepper in a medium skillet. Heat and stir on boiling until boiling. Add meatballs. Heat and stir for about 1 minute until glazed.

Bison meat is leaner and has fewer calories than beef but is still packed with iron and protein and is a source of omega-3 fatty acids. Although it is not as common as beef, bison meat is starting to turn up in many grocery stores as well as at farmers' markets throughout the province.

Coffee and Chocolate Braised Short Ribs

Serves 6

Short ribs have not always been the darling staple of top restaurants. This cut of meat has lots of fat, bone and connective tissue and was once considered "what was left" after the choice cuts of beef were taken. However, some simple kitchen magic entailing trimming and a long, moist cooking method results in meat that is tender, rich and tasty. There are lots of short rib recipes calling for a wine-based braising liquid, but because Vancouver has such a strong coffee culture, we felt some java would be an appropriate substitution. Use any good, strong coffee that is not too bitter and combine it with your favourite dark chocolate for a unique dish that will have your friends coming back for more.

¼ cup (60 mL) olive oil

5 lbs (2.3 kg) beef short ribs

sea salt and freshly ground pepper

1 large onion, chopped

1 large red pepper, chopped

1 large jalapeño pepper, seeded and finely chopped

4 cloves garlic, minced

2 Tbsp (30 mL) dark brown sugar

2 Tbsp (30 mL) ancho chile powder

¼ cup (60 mL) fresh oregano, chopped

1 tsp (5 mL) cumin

2 cups (500 mL) strong coffee

1 x 28 oz (796 mL) can diced tomatoes in juice

1 Tbsp (15 mL) tomato paste

1 cup (250 mL) dark, unsweetened chocolate, at least 70% cocoa, shaved

chopped fresh cilantro

Preheat oven to 300° F (150° C). Heat oil in a heavy-bottomed pot over medium-high. Season short ribs with salt and pepper. Working in batches, sear short ribs in oil until nicely browned and transfer to a platter.

Reduce heat to medium and add onions and peppers to oil and drippings in pot, stirring until onions are translucent. Stir in garlic and sauté for 1 minute. Add brown sugar, ancho chile powder, oregano and cumin and cook for 5 minutes. Stir in coffee, tomatoes and tomato paste and bring the mixture to a boil. Add short ribs and collected juices to pot and heat until boiling.

Cover and bake in oven until meat is very tender, about 1¾ to 2 hours. Stir in chocolate until it is melted and evenly distributed in sauce. Season to taste with salt and pepper and garnish with cilantro. Serve with Smashed Pemberton Fingerlings with Fresh Herbs and Truffle Oil (see p. 110).

Ancho chiles are dried poblano peppers and are known for their mild heat and sweet flavour. They are common in Mexican cooking, particularly in tamales.

Gnocchi in a Sorrel Sauce

Serves 2 as a main course, 4 as a side dish

Gnocchi, which means "dumplings" in Italian, are one of the most versatile Italian dishes. Commonly made using potato and semolina flour, these little balls should be as light as air. They work well with a variety of sauces, including this tasty sorrel sauce, but also try variations, including creamy blue cheese, truffles or even just a simple meat sauce. The secret to gnocchi is to not overcook them because they will start to fall apart. As with all Italian pasta dishes, *al dente*, or "tender to the tooth," is the desired doneness.

1 lb (500 g) package gnocchi

splash of olive oil

1 Tbsp (15 mL) unsalted butter

1 small shallot, minced

½ cup (125 mL) white wine

1 cup (250 mL) heavy cream (32%)

1 packed cup (250 g) sorrel, chopped

¼ cup (60 mL) parsley, chopped

sea salt and freshly ground pepper to taste

fresh chives, chopped

freshly grated Parmesan cheese

Bring a big pot of salted water to a rolling boil and cook gnocchi until they float to surface. Drain, toss with a splash of olive oil and set aside.

In a large saucepan, heat butter and add shallot. Cook for 2 to 3 minutes, then add white wine and cook until wine has reduced by half. Add cream and continue cooking for 5 minutes at medium-high heat.

Purée sorrel and parsley in a blender along with hot cream mixture until everything is incorporated; sauce will turn a jade green colour. Pour sauce back into pan along with gnocchi to heat through and season with salt and pepper. Serve in warm bowls with chives and Parmesan cheese sprinkled on top.

〰️ *Gnocchi are often made using potatoes, but they can also be made with durum wheat, flour or ricotta cheese. Traditionally, gnocchi are served with tomato sauce or melted butter and Parmesan cheese, but they lend themselves well to almost any sauce.*

Birch Syrup Roasted Squash Ravioli with Brown Butter Hazelnut Sauce

Serves 6

Birch syrup is one of BC's best-kept secrets. Like maple syrup, birch syrup is made using the reduced sap from its mother tree. However, the main difference between birch and maple syrup is that it takes double the amount of sap from a birch tree to make the same amount of syrup; incredibly, this means 85 to 105 quarts (80 to 100 L) of sap must be collected to make 1 quart (1 L) of syrup! As a result, birch syrup is nearly five times the price of maple syrup. Don't let this deter you from splurging on this unique syrup from northern BC to complement Similkameen Valley squash and Fraser Valley hazelnuts for a truly British Columbian fall dish.

½ cup (125 mL) unsalted butter, *divided*

½ small onion, diced

1 cup (250 mL) roasted butternut squash purée (see opposite)

sea salt and freshly ground pepper to taste

3 Tbsp (45 mL) heavy cream (32%)

3 Tbsp (45 mL) grated Parmesan cheese, plus more for topping

pinch of nutmeg

1 recipe pasta dough, rolled out into wide ribbons (see p. 21)

½ cup (125 mL) roughly chopped hazelnuts

1 Tbsp (15 mL) finely chopped fresh parsley leaves

In a large pan, melt 1 Tbsp (15 mL) of butter and sauté onions over medium heat. Add butternut squash purée and cook until mixture is slightly dry, about 2 to 3 minutes. Season with salt and pepper. Stir in cream and continue to cook for 2 minutes. Remove from heat and stir in Parmesan cheese and nutmeg, and adjust salt and pepper, if needed. Set the filling aside to cool completely.

Set a large pot of salted water to boil. Cut pasta ribbons into 3 in (7.5 cm) squares. Place 2 tsp (10 mL) of filling in centre of each ravioli square. Using a pastry brush, lightly brush edges of pasta with water and cover with a second square. Press edges slightly to seal. If desired, you can cut pasta into circles with a round cookie cutter. Add ravioli to pot of boiling water and cook until al dente, about 2 to 3 minutes, or until they are paler in colour and float to surface. With a slotted spoon, remove ravioli from water and drain well.

In a large pan, melt remaining butter over medium-high heat, add hazelnuts and continue to cook until butter starts to brown. Remove from heat, and toss ravioli in butter. Place ravioli in centre of each serving plate and spoon any remaining butter sauce and hazelnuts on top. Sprinkle Parmesan cheese over pasta and garnish with parsley.

Preheat oven to 375° F (190° C). Cut butternut squash in half lengthwise, scoop out seeds and place flesh side up on a baking pan. Pour birch syrup on top, season lightly with salt and pepper and bake in oven for 45 minutes or until tender when pierced with a fork. Cool, scoop out flesh and mash.

Birch Syrup Butternut Squash Purée

1 x 1 lb (500g) butternut squash

⅓ cup (75 mL) birch syrup

sea salt and fresh ground pepper

Smashed Pemberton Fingerlings with Fresh Herbs and Truffle Oil

Serves 6

Combining two great earthy ingredients—Pemberton fingerling potatoes and aromatic truffle oil—makes for a heavenly combination of flavours. Truffle oil is made by infusing good quality oil (usually olive), with luxurious Italian white or black truffles. The oil absorbs the aroma and flavour of the pungent fungi and turns ordinary smashed potatoes into something that tastes elegantly divine. And don't just use truffle oil for potatoes, try it with BC free-range eggs, Okanagan goat cheese or even local Chilliwack popping corn!

2 lbs (1 kg) fingerling potatoes

¼ cup (60 mL) butter, sliced

3 Tbsp (45 mL) heavy cream (32%)

⅓ cup (75 mL) sour cream

sea salt and freshly ground pepper to taste

¼ cup (60 mL) fresh herbs (such as thyme, rosemary, tarragon or dill)

truffle oil for drizzling

In a large pot, cover potatoes with salted water and bring to a boil over high heat. Reduce to medium-high and cook until potatoes are tender when pricked with a fork, about 15 minutes. Drain and return potatoes to pot.

Add butter and cream to potatoes, and smash potatoes into uneven chunks with a large fork or potato masher. Mix in sour cream and fresh herbs, and season with salt and pepper. Drizzle truffle oil on top of potatoes and serve.

Roasted Jerusalem Artichokes

Serves 4 as a side dish

Also known as "sunchokes" and "Canada's potatoes," Jerusalem artichokes are easy to grow and even produce a display of small sunflowers in late summer. In BC, Jerusalem artichokes are best harvested in fall when light frosts enhance their natural sweetness. Native to North America, Jerusalem artichokes have waxy flesh that is the texture of a crispy apple, and their flavour is reminiscent of sunflower seeds. Traditionally, the tubers were simply boiled and eaten much like potatoes, and they can be used in place of potatoes in many recipes. They also make excellent soups!

4 cloves garlic, chopped

2½ Tbsp (37 mL) extra virgin olive oil

1½ lbs (680 g) Jerusalem artichokes

sea salt and freshly ground black pepper to taste

1 Tbsp (15 mL) chopped fresh parsley

Preheat oven to 350° F (175° C). Heat garlic and oil in a small pot and cook until soft. Peel Jerusalem artichokes and cut into small chunks, placing chunks into a bowl of acidulated water (see Tip) as you work. Put chokes in a shallow roasting pan large enough to hold everything in one layer comfortably. Strain garlic from oil and pour oil over chokes. Add salt and pepper and toss.

Bake in oven for about 20 minutes, stirring once or twice, until tender. Sprinkle parsley on top and serve.

The Jerusalem artichoke has no ties to the famous Biblical city; the name simply comes from the English misunderstanding the Italian word girasol, *which means "sunflower."*

Tip

Acidulated water is just water to which a little acid—
normally lemon or lime juice or vinegar—has been added;
½ tsp (2 mL) per cup (250 mL) is enough. When you are
peeling or cutting fruits or vegetables that discolour quickly
when exposed to air, like apples, place them in acidulated
water to prevent browning. Jerusalem artichokes, globe
artichokes and salsify are just some of the foods that
benefit from this treatment. Acidulated water is also
sometimes used for cooking.

Brussels Sprouts with Pancetta and Pine Nuts

Serves 6

Because they do well in cool climates, Brussels sprouts are perfectly suited to BC; they even improve in flavour, sweetness and tenderness if allowed to chill through the first few frosts. Brussels sprouts came originally from the region around Afghanistan and, like cauliflower, are actually a variety of cabbage. Because Brussels sprouts are often overcooked, they do not hold a place among the stars of the vegetable kingdom (nor at many dinner tables), which is a shame. Try this recipe with goose prosciutto or even prosciutto "bits" from Oyama Sausage at Granville Island.

2 lbs (1 kg) Brussels sprouts

splash of olive oil

5 oz (140 g) pancetta or prosciutto, diced

sea salt and freshly ground pepper to taste

½ cup (125 mL) pine nuts, toasted (see Tip)

Preheat oven to 400° F (205° C). Slice Brussels sprouts in half lengthwise, removing any loose outer leaves and trimming bottom stems. Toss in olive oil and add pancetta or prosciutto, salt and pepper. Spread in a single layer on a baking sheet and bake for 20 to 30 minutes until pancetta or prosciutto is crispy. Stir occasionally, so the Brussels sprouts cook evenly. Toss with pine nuts and another splash of olive oil, if desired.

Tip

To toast pine nuts, place in a dry skillet and cook on low heat, stirring occasionally, until lightly golden.

Pancetta is Italian bacon and is available at most delis and Italian markets.

Tamarind Vegetable Curry

Serves 4 to 6

Tamarind may not be a common ingredient in much of Canada's cuisine, but it is widely used in Indian cooking, lending a distinctly sour taste to the dishes. Tamarind is native to eastern Africa and grows throughout India, Southeast Asia and the West Indies. You are not likely to see any tamarind trees growing wild in BC, but thanks to the province's large Indian community (second largest in Canada, after Toronto) you can still get your hands on the pulp; check your local Asian market. This sweet and tangy dish is reminiscent of chutney, rich with curry and mustard seed. It is a hot and sour side that's right at home in a lavish spread of Indian plates such as poppadum, basmati rice and some tasty meat dishes.

2 Tbsp (30 mL) ghee

1 tsp (5 mL) brown mustard seed

1 tsp (5 mL) cumin seed

1½ cups (375 mL) chopped onion

2 Tbsp (30 mL) finely grated ginger root

4 garlic cloves, minced

2 Tbsp (30 mL) hot curry paste

1½ cups (375 mL) cubed, peeled orange-fleshed sweet potato, cut in ½ inch (12 mm) pieces

1 cup (250 mL) cubed butternut squash, cut in ½ inch (12 mm) pieces

2 cups (500 mL) chopped fresh green beans

¾ cup (175 mL) tamarind liquid (see opposite)

3 Tbsp (45 mL) brown sugar, packed

1 tsp (5 mL) salt

½ tsp (2 mL) pepper

Heat ghee in a skillet on medium. Add mustard and cumin seed and stir for 15 seconds until mustard seed pops. Add onion, ginger and garlic and cook for 5 minutes until onion is softened. Add curry paste and stir for 1 minute. Add sweet potato and squash, and cook for 10 minutes stirring occasionally, until potato starts to brown. Add green beans, tamarind liquid, brown sugar, salt and pepper and bring to a boil. Cook, covered, for 8 minutes until potato and squash are tender.

Tip

When choosing a curry paste for this recipe, be sure to purchase it at an Asian market and choose an Indian paste (as opposed to Thai). Don't be shy to ask the staff for assistance in choosing one that suits your palate—curry pastes range from mild to very, very hot!

How to Make Tamarind Liquid

Measure the amount of chopped tamarind pulp that corresponds to the desired yield (see chart, below) and put into a small bowl. Pour the appropriate amount of boiling water over the pulp. Stir to break up pulp and let stand for 5 minutes. Press through a fine sieve and discard solids.

Liquid Yield	Pulp Amount	Water Amount
1 Tbsp (15 mL)	1 Tbsp (15 mL)	3 Tbsp (45 mL)
2 Tbsp (30 mL)	2 Tbsp (30 mL)	1/4 cup (60 mL)
3 Tbsp (45 mL)	2 Tbsp (30 mL)	1/3 cup (75 mL)
1/2 cup (125 mL)	1/4 cup (60 mL)	3/4 cup (175 mL)
3/4 cup (175 mL)	1/3 cup (75 mL)	1 cup (250 mL)
1 cup (250 mL)	1/2 cup (125 mL)	1 1/2 cups (375 mL)

Ghee is clarified butter (the milk solids have been removed) and is commonly used in Indian cooking. Without the milk solids, butter has a much higher smoke point but does not lose that great flavour. You can either make your own ghee or buy it in most Asian markets.

Apple Pear Chutney

Makes 4 cups (1 L)

Foodies in BC are enamoured with chutneys and jams that pair well with cheese plates, roasted meats and more. This recipe, with its enticing combination of fresh apple and sweet pear, meets the bill perfectly. Fresh apples are available in BC from August to October, right when pears are plentiful and in season. Pears, unlike most other fruit, are picked before they are ripe because if left on the tree to ripen, they become mushy around the core.

2 tsp (10 mL) canola oil

½ cup (125 mL) chopped onion

¼ tsp (1 mL) ground allspice

¼ tsp (1 mL) ground cinnamon

⅛ tsp (0.5 mL) ground cloves

⅛ tsp (0.5 ml) ground nutmeg

3 cups (750 mL) chopped, peeled apple, such as McIntosh

2 cups (500 mL) chopped, peeled pear

1 cup (250 mL) apple juice

⅓ cup (75 mL) brown sugar, packed

¼ cup (60 mL) apple cider vinegar

¼ cup (60 mL) raisins

Heat canola oil in a medium saucepan on medium. Add onion, allspice, cinnamon, cloves and nutmeg. Cook for about 5 minutes, stirring often, until onion is caramelized. Add apple, pear, apple juice, brown sugar, vinegar and raisins, and bring to a boil. Boil gently, uncovered, for about 6 minutes, stirring occasionally, until apple and pear are just tender. Remove from heat. Transfer 1 cup (250 mL) to a blender and carefully process with on/off motion for about 1 minute until chunky. Return to apple mixture and stir. Fill 4 hot, sterile 1 cup (250 mL) jars to within ½ inch (12 mm) of top. Wipe rims and place sterile metal lids on jars, then screw on metal bands fingertip tight. Do not over-tighten. Process in boiling water bath for 15 minutes. Remove jars and let stand at room temperature until cool. Store in refrigerator for up to 1 month after opening.

Tip

Pears ripen from the inside out, so you can't necessarily judge the ripeness by the colour; if you can jiggle the stem of a pear, it is ripe.

Fruit Smoothie

Serves 1

A fruit smoothie is a great, healthy breakfast for people on the go. Smoothies are the perfect excuse (although who needs one?) to use some of BC's yummiest treats—from fruit such as blueberries, strawberries or peaches, to yogurt from Island Farms or Birchwood Dairy, to honey from Chilliwack River Valley Natural Honey Ltd. Some of our favourite smoothy combinations include peach, pineapple and coconut and blueberry banana. Smoothies can also be made using frozen yogurt, frozen bananas, ice cream or even soy milk. Try a shot of Baileys Irish Cream in a chocolate banana smoothie for a weekend indulgence.

1 banana, peeled and frozen

¾ cup (175 mL) fresh or frozen berries

¼ cup (60 mL) coconut milk

1 cup (250 mL) vanilla soy milk

1 Tbsp (15 mL) almond butter

¼ cup (60 mL) crushed ice

Purée all ingredients in a blender until smooth.

Tip
Coconut milk from a can will keep in the fridge for 4 to 5 days.

Blossom Cups with Jicama Shrimp Filling

Makes 12

These delicate blossoms appear innocuous—but looks are deceiving. The crisp wrappers surround a blend of shrimp, crunchy carrot and jicama garnished with fiery hot peppers. This is a great dish for holiday parties or gatherings at home any time of the year. Be sure to choose West Coast shrimp or prawns that are from a sustainable source.

6 egg roll wrappers (8 in [20 cm] square), cut into quarters

¼ cup (60 mL) + 1 tsp (5 mL) canola oil, *divided*

1 tsp (5 mL) sesame oil

½ lb (225 g) uncooked shrimp (peeled and deveined), chopped

1 tsp (5 mL) finely grated ginger root

1 garlic clove, minced

2 cups (500 mL) julienned jicama

1 cup (250 mL) julienned carrot

1 Tbsp (15 mL) sweet chili sauce

¼ tsp (1 mL) salt

Make 1 in (2.5 cm) cuts halfway along each side of wrappers. Combine ¼ cup (60 mL) canola oil and sesame oil and brush onto 1 side of wrappers. Press 12 wrappers, oil side down, into 12 muffin cups. Press a second wrapper, oil side down, into each muffin cup, alternating points to form a flower shape. Bake in a 425° F (220° C) oven for 4 minutes until golden and crisp. Let stand in pan on wire rack for 5 minutes. Gently remove from pan.

Heat remaining canola oil in a wok or large skillet on medium-high. Add shrimp, ginger and garlic and stir-fry for 1 minute until shrimp is pink. Transfer to a bowl.

Add jicama, carrot, chili sauce and salt to wok and stir-fry for 5 minutes until vegetables are tender-crisp. Return shrimp to wok and stir. Spoon into cups.

Grilled Asian Pears and Avocado Salad with Lemongrass and Garam Masala Vinaigrette

Serves 4

At one time, Asian or Indian food ingredients were only available in specialty ethnic markets. Now, with the rising popularity of ethnic cuisine and the proliferation of multi-ethnic communities in BC, these once hard-to-find ingredients are available in local grocery stores throughout the province. This recipe combines both Asian and Indian flavours to create a mouth-watering salad using the fresh citrus flavour of lemongrass and the heady aroma of garam masala. Although we prefer to use Vij's own garam masala blend, which you can purchase at his restaurant or at other gourmet retailers in Vancouver, any blend will work fine. The other secret to this recipe is the grilled avocado—once you have tried it, you will never eat an ungrilled avocado again.

¼ cup (60 mL) canola oil

2 Tbsp (30 mL) honey

2 Asian pears, halved

2 avocados, peeled, halved and cut into 4 slices

sea salt and freshly ground pepper

Garam Masala Vinaigrette

¼ cup (60 mL) garam masala paste

⅓ cup (75 mL) oil

¼ cup (60 mL) rice wine vinegar

2 stalks of lemongrass, finely minced

½ lb (250 g) baby salad greens

Mix oil and honey together in a small bowl. Brush on Asian pears and avocados and grill over medium heat for about 5 minutes. Season with salt and pepper.

For vinaigrette, whisk garam masala paste, oil, rice wine vinegar and lemongrass together in a small bowl. Drizzle vinaigrette over salad greens, toss lightly and serve on individual plates with pears and avocado.

〰 *The Asian pear is slightly rounder than the familiar Bartlett pear, and considerably juicier. Asian pears offer a sweet-and-sour sensation that's similar to pineapple.*

Potato and Roasted Garlic Chowder

Serves 4

Garlic has long been reputed to prevent everything from the common cold and flu to the plague. Besides this, it makes almost everything taste good—including ordinary potato chowder. Roasting whole garlic neutralizes its pungency and brings out its sweetness; local BC potatoes are a perfect foil to its mellow flavour. Delicious and nutritious, this soup is sure to ward off the usual wintertime ailments. Stop by your local winter farmers' market and find some Okanagan or Similkameen Valley garlic, with large bulbs that are perfect for roasting.

2 medium onions, diced

¼ cup (60 mL) unsalted butter

1 Tbsp (15 mL) olive oil

2 cups (500 mL) celery, diced

1 cup (250 mL) carrots, diced

4 medium potatoes, peeled and diced

1 bay leaf

vegetable or chicken stock, enough to just cover vegetables

2 bulbs roasted garlic (see above), cloves squeezed out and roughly chopped

2 cups (500 mL) heavy cream (32%)

sea salt and freshly ground pepper to taste

¼ cup (60 mL) fresh herbs such as parsley, thyme or mint, chopped

In a heavy pot, sauté onions in butter and oil until they turn golden. Add celery, carrots, potatoes and bay leaf and cover with stock. Simmer for 15 minutes, then add roasted garlic and cream, and simmer for 10 to 15 minutes more or until the potatoes are cooked and the soup is reduced and creamy. Season to taste with salt and pepper. Ladle soup into bowls and garnish with a sprinkle of herbs.

Kitsilano Maple Cream Ale and Cheddar Soup

Serves 4

It doesn't get more Canadian than maple syrup and beer. Beer and maple syrup? This interesting flavour combination is uniquely West Coast, thanks to Granville Island Brewing, which opened its doors in 1984 as one of Canada's first microbreweries and continues today as a leader in BC's microbrew industry. One of its most popular beers to date is the Kitsilano Maple Cream Ale, which combines pure Canadian maple syrup with its traditional hand-crafted beer. There is no better beer for this hearty winter soup, featuring another Canadian favourite: Cheddar cheese.

2 medium onions, diced

¼ cup (60 mL) unsalted butter

1 Tbsp (15 mL) olive oil

2 cups (500 mL) celery, diced

1 cup (250 mL) parsnips, diced

4 medium potatoes, peeled and diced

1 bay leaf

vegetable or chicken stock, enough to just cover vegetables

2 cups (500 mL) heavy cream (32%)

2 cups (500 mL) sharp white Cheddar cheese, grated

½ to 1 bottle of Warthog Ale (or your choice of brown ale), about 6 to 12 oz (170 to 341 mL) or to taste

sea salt and freshly ground pepper

In a heavy pot, sauté onions in butter and oil until they turn golden. Add celery, parsnips, potatoes, bay leaf and enough stock to cover everything. Simmer for 15 minutes, then add cream and simmer for 10 to 15 minutes more or until potatoes are cooked and soup is reduced and creamy. Remove soup from heat and blend in cheese in small batches. Purée soup in a blender, then return to medium-low heat and stir in ale to taste. Season with salt and pepper and serve.

Canadians spend over $6.7 billion per year on beer, accounting for more than 51% of the sales of all alcohol combined.

Cioppino with Fennel and Saffron

Serves 6

Cioppino is an Italian seafood stew whose North American roots are thought to have originated in the San Francisco Bay area when Italian immigrants from Genoa replaced traditional Genoese ingredients with the fresh fish available to them on the West Coast. Most Italians who came to Canada before World War II came by way of the United States and brought with them this cioppino. The combination of BC's abundance of fresh, local seafood and the large Italian district of Commercial Drive, located on the east side of Vancouver, means that a good bowl of cioppino is not hard to find; just be sure to ask for a bib because it can be a deliciously messy experience!

2 lbs (1 kg) snapper fillet, cleaned

1 lb (500 g) fresh shrimp, tails on

½ lb (250 g) each clams, mussels and scallops

1 crab, cooked, cleaned and cracked

2 Tbsp (30 mL) extra virgin olive oil

1 small onion, minced

1 medium fennel bulb, diced

1 cup (250 mL) white wine

3 cloves garlic, minced

zest from half an orange, minced

pinch of saffron, or to taste, dissolved in ¼ cup (60 mL) warm stock

4 cups (1 L) tomato sauce

3 cups (750 mL) fish stock

sea salt and freshly ground pepper

½ cup (125 mL) fresh basil

(continued on next page)

Wash all fish and seafood, except crab, and pat dry. In a heavy-bottomed pot, heat oil and sauté onion. Stir in fennel and sauté for 5 minutes. Add wine and garlic, and simmer for 10 minutes. Stir in orange zest, saffron, tomato sauce and stock, and simmer for 10 minutes. Nestle fish fillets and seafood into sauce, making sure to cover them with liquid. Cover, bring back to a simmer over medium-high heat and cook until clams and mussels open, about 10 to 12 minutes. Season with salt and pepper. Serve hot in warmed bowls, garnished with fresh basil.

Tip

It is traditional to serve cioppino with polenta and a bottle of Chianti.

Bring milk and cream to a boil. Whisk in polenta and cook, stirring continuously, for 20 minutes. Season to taste with salt and pepper. Serve hot topped with mascarpone. You can also pour polenta into a rectangular baking dish. Once cooled, it can be sliced and pan-grilled with butter.

Tip

If you have trouble finding polenta and mascarpone, try an Italian deli.

Polenta with Mascarpone

4 cups (1 L) milk

½ cup (125 mL) heavy cream (32%)

1 cup (250 mL) polenta

sea salt and freshly ground pepper to taste

1 cup (250 mL) mascarpone

Mussels with White Wine and Garlic

Serves 4 to 6

Fresh mussels steamed in white wine is a natural BC dish, but local mussels are hard to come by because they are also a favourite delicacy of ducks, raccoons and even starfish! If you get an opportunity, try to find BC Honey or Gallo Mussels, which are harvested in places such as Redonda, Salt Spring and Cortes Islands. These mussels are large and have rich, plump meat. However, because of their rarity, you will usually only find them on restaurant menus, and even then only as an appetizer portion thanks to their high price. BC only began seriously cultivating mussels in 1999, so this young industry will surely grow in the coming years.

4 lbs (2 kg) mussels

1 cup (250 mL) white wine such as Chardonnay

4 cloves garlic, minced

1 Tbsp (15 mL) butter

¼ cup (60 mL) chives, chopped

Scrub mussels under cool running water and remove any beards. Discard mussels that don't close when gently tapped.

Place white wine and garlic in a large pot and bring to a boil. Add mussels to pot, cover and reduce heat, cooking for about 5 to 6 minutes. Discard any mussels that have not opened. With a slotted spoon transfer mussels into serving dishes.

Turn heat to high and bring remaining liquid to a boil. Cook for 2 to 3 minutes, until it has reduced slightly, and whisk in butter. Spoon sauce over mussels, sprinkle with chives and serve hot.

Tip

Use your fresh mussels within 24 hours of purchasing them. The best way to store fresh mussels is to put them in a colander and place the colander into a bowl. Cover the mussels with ice and then with a damp towel. The mussels will stay very cold and have good air circulation, without being submerged (or drowned) in water.

Blackened Trout with Oven-dried Tomatoes

Serves 2

A favourite pastime for many BC residents during the warmer months of the year is heading out to fish on one of the many lakes that dot the province. Nothing tastes better than a breakfast of pan-fried trout with brown butter and eggs cooked over an open fire. However, for those winter evenings when you are in the comfort of your own home, many local fishmongers sell excellent farm-raised trout that will bring back those summer memories. The blackening spices in this recipe will warm you up, and the oven-dried tomatoes are a hearty version of the sweet, vine-ripened summer variety. You can even plan ahead next summer and dry your own heirloom tomatoes for recipes such as this.

2 lbs (1 kg) Roma tomatoes, halved lengthwise

3 cloves garlic, minced

¼ cup (60 mL) fresh thyme, chopped

sea salt and freshly ground black pepper to taste

½ cup (125 mL) extra virgin olive oil

Spice Mixture

2 tsp (10 mL) paprika

2 tsp (10 mL) chipotle powder or chili powder

2 tsp (10 mL) ground cumin

2 tsp (10 mL) dried thyme

1 tsp (5 mL) freshly ground black pepper

1 tsp (5 mL) sea salt

2 fresh trout, gutted but whole

2 Tbsp (30 mL) canola oil

Preheat oven to 250° F (120° C). Scoop seeds out of tomatoes. Mix garlic with thyme, salt, pepper and olive oil. Place tomatoes cut side up in a roasting pan and drizzle with garlic mixture. Bake for at least 3 hours or until tomatoes are dehydrated but still chewy.

Mix all spices together in a bowl.

Rinse trout with water and pat dry with paper towels. Brush canola oil on trout and rub it all over with spice mixture.

Heat canola oil in a heavy-bottomed skillet until it is smoking hot. Place prepared trout in skillet, cook for 2 to 4 minutes and turn over. Cook until fish is firm and cooked through, 3 to 4 minutes. Use a fork to test doneness—fish should flake easily but should not be dry. Serve with oven-dried tomatoes on side.

Tip

Oven-drying tomatoes is a great way to
preserve these tasty bits of summer
sunshine. Any leftover tomatoes can be
covered in olive oil and stored in a jar. They
will keep for up to 3 weeks refrigerated.

Sloping Hill Farm Hazelnut-roasted Pork with Birch Syrup

Serves 8 to 10

The majority of BC's pork production—about 80%—takes place in the Fraser Valley, but the North Okanagan and Vancouver Island also play a significant role. Specialty farmers such as Sloping Hill Farm on Vancouver Island are raising the bar for locally produced organic pork by using free-range pens, limiting the number of animals and encouraging natural behaviour. By using local pork, hazelnuts and birch syrup, this recipe is truly a testament to the best of the province.

Stuffing

2 Tbsp (30 mL) olive oil

1 onion, finely chopped

4 cloves garlic, roughly chopped

¼ cup (60 mL) fresh rosemary, chopped

¼ cup (60 mL) fresh thyme, chopped

2 cups (500 mL) hazelnuts, roughly chopped

¼ cup (60 mL) chicken stock

2 Tbsp (30 mL) dry breadcrumbs

1 Tbsp (15 mL) dark brown sugar

2 x 3 lb (1.4 kg) pork loin rib roast, patted dry, room temperature

sea salt and freshly ground pepper

3 to 6 sprigs of fresh rosemary

1 Tbsp (15 mL) olive oil

(continued on next page)

Preheat oven to 400° F (205° C).

For stuffing, heat 2 Tbsp (30 mL) of olive oil in a pan and cook onions, garlic, rosemary and thyme for a few minutes. Add hazelnuts. Stir in chicken stock, breadcrumbs and brown sugar, and set stuffing aside.

Turn pork loin rib roast fat side down. Slit lengthwise, almost but not quite all the way through, to form a long pocket, leaving a ½ in (1 cm) border of uncut meat at each end. Sprinkle generously with salt and pepper. Fill cavity with stuffing. Tie loin together with butcher twine or heavy-duty kitchen string at 1½ in (3 to 4 cm) intervals. Slide rosemary sprigs under twine. Brush with remaining olive oil and sprinkle generously with salt and pepper. Set, fat side up, diagonally or curved (so it fits) on a large baking sheet or jelly roll pan.

Canada is one of the world's largest pork exporters, shipping products to more than 140 countries.

For glaze, mix birch syrup, white wine and chicken broth together. Brush glaze mixture on meat.

Roast in oven until a meat thermometer registers 150 to 155° F (65 to 68° C), about 2 hours, occasionally brushing with pan drippings. Let roast rest 15 to 20 minutes out of oven, then transfer to a carving board.

To make sauce, stir juices around pan to loosen browned bits. Pour through a strainer into a small pan, and stir in port and chicken stock. Bring to simmer and cook until slightly thickened. Slice pork roast and serve with sauce.

Glaze

½ cup (125 mL) birch syrup

¼ cup (60 mL) white wine, preferably a Riesling

¼ cup (60 mL) chicken broth

Sauce

¼ cup (60 mL) port

¼ cup (60 mL) chicken stock

Grilled Quail with Pistachio and Pomegranate

Serves 4

Quail belongs to a family of game birds that were vital to the survival of both native peoples and early settlers. You can see quail both in the wild and on signage for local businesses throughout the province's Okanagan region. Although many of these birds are spotted running across the roads, most game birds consumed in BC's are raised in captivity. Known for their rich, moist meat, quail are the most popular of the small game birds, with more than 350,000 being produced annually. Other game birds being raised include pheasants, partridge, squab and silkies. While quail are frequently offered on the menus of upscale restaurants, they are also available for the home cook in specialty shops and meat markets.

Marinade

½ clove garlic, minced

1 tsp (5 mL) cinnamon

1 tsp (5 mL) cumin

½ onion, finely chopped

3 Tbsp (45 mL) pomegranate molasses

juice from half a lime

4 quail, cut through backbone and flattened out

sea salt and freshly ground pepper

Sauce

1 cup (250 mL) bacon, diced

½ garlic clove, minced

¼ cup (60 mL) pomegranate molasses

½ cup (125 mL) pistachios, whole

sea salt and freshly ground pepper to taste

arugula leaves for garnish

In a large bowl, prepare marinade and toss to combine.

Season each quail with salt and pepper and place in marinade. Cover and refrigerate for at least 1 hour and up to 24 hours.

For sauce, sauté bacon in a pan until crispy. Remove all fat drippings except for 1 Tbsp (15 mL). Add garlic, pomegranate molasses, pistachios, salt and pepper and heat through.

Grill quail over medium-high heat for about 7 minutes each side, or until juices run clear. Serve on a bed of arugula leaves with sauce drizzled on top.

Pomegranate molasses is a syrup made from cooked-down pomegranate juice. It can be found in Middle Eastern stores.

Eggplant Lasagna

Serves 6 to 8

Eggplant (*Solanum melongena*), like its cousin the tomato, was long believed to be poisonous (well, more accurately, thought to drive people mad) and got off to a slow start in gardens outside of the Mediterranean, except as an ornamental plant. Eggplant is unique in the nightshade family as the only member to have originated in the Eastern Hemisphere—in India and China specifically. Like tomatoes, peppers and potatoes, eggplants come in a wide variety of shapes and colours, although globe-shaped varieties such as "Black Beauty" are most common in grocery stores here. Eggplant got its name because early varieties introduced to Europe were white and looked like eggs!

1 eggplant, sliced ½ inch (1 cm) thick, crosswise

1 medium zucchini, sliced ½ inch (1 cm) thick

2 to 3 Tbsp (30 to 45 mL) olive oil

sea salt and freshly ground pepper to taste

Tomato Sauce

1 Tbsp (15 mL) olive oil

2 Tbsp (30 mL) butter

2 large onions, finely chopped

3 or 4 cloves garlic, minced

2 bay leaves

splash of red wine

2 cups (500 mL) canned plum tomatoes, roughly chopped

12 sheets oven-ready lasagna noodles

2 cups (500 mL) freshly grated Asiago cheese

(continued on next page)

Toss eggplant and zucchini slices with olive oil and season with salt and pepper. Grill on a stovetop grill or barbecue for 5 minutes on each side. Set aside.

Preheat oven to 375° F (190° C). For sauce, warm oil and butter in a heavy-based casserole over medium heat. Add onion and sauté for about 5 minutes until softened and translucent. Add garlic and cook for another couple of minutes, stirring to coat well. Cook gently for about 5 minutes. Add bay leaves, salt and pepper. Pour in wine and simmer until it has evaporated, then add tomatoes with their juice and stir thoroughly. Cook, uncovered, for 30 minutes. Taste and correct seasoning.

For ricotta mixture, combine ingredients in medium bowl. Season to taste and set aside.

For béchamel, pour milk into a saucepan with bay leaves, onion and a generous pinch of nutmeg. Bring to just below boiling point, then remove from heat and leave to infuse for 10 minutes. Strain milk to remove bay leaves and onion. Melt butter in a saucepan and stir in flour. Cook, stirring, for 5 minutes. Pour hot milk into flour mixture. Cook on low heat, stirring frequently, for 10 minutes until thickened. Season sauce with salt and pepper and set aside.

To assemble, start by buttering a 13 x 9 x 3 in (33 x 23 x 5 cm) baking pan. Pour some béchamel into baking pan—enough to just cover bottom. Top with a layer of lasagna, add béchamel, a layer of grilled vegetables, tomato sauce, then more béchamel and a good handful of Asiago cheese. Cover with lasagna, then ricotta mixture. Top with lasagna, then béchamel, vegetables, tomato sauce. Add another layer of lasagna and top with béchamel. Add a final sprinkling of Asiago cheese. Bake for 30 to 40 minutes, until browned and bubbling all over.

Tip

Older eggplants will have an acrid flavour, so choose freshly picked, if possible. Alternatively, you can remove most of the bitter flavour by salting the sliced eggplant and letting it sit for 10 to 15 minutes. Gently squeeze out the bitter liquid, rinse lightly in cold water and pat dry on paper towel.

Tip

You can add as many layers as you wish, depending on the size of your pan.

Ricotta Mixture

2 cups (500 mL) ricotta cheese

½ cup (125 mL) freshly grated Parmesan cheese

½ cup (125 mL) freshly grated Mozzarella cheese

sea salt and freshly ground pepper

Béchamel

3 cups (750 mL) milk

2 bay leaves

1 onion, halved

pinch of freshly grated nutmeg

¼ cup (60 mL) butter

¼ cup (60 mL) flour

sea salt and freshly ground pepper

Tempura

Makes about 2¼ cups (550 mL) tempura batter

Batter-laced deep-frying is a method of cooking that was introduced to Japan by Portuguese missionaries during the 16th century. By the 17th century, Tokyo street vendors were selling tempura, using fish freshly caught in Tokyo Bay and most often fried in sesame oil. This traditional cooking method has caught on in BC thanks to the huge interest in Japanese cuisine. It is now more common to have sushi days in elementary schools than hot dog days! This is a simple recipe that will please every member of your family. Be sure to choose the freshest possible ingredients, such as BC spot prawns, salmon, squash and even zucchini blossoms.

peanut oil

1 egg, beaten

1 cup (250 mL) cold beer

2 Tbsp (30 mL) dry white wine

½ cup (125 mL) flour

¼ cup (60 mL) rice flour

¼ cup (60 mL) cornstarch

variety of vegetables and seafood, cut into bite-sized pieces

Heat peanut oil in a pan or deep fryer until temperature is 375° F (190° C). Combine egg, beer and white wine in a small bowl. In another bowl, combine flour, rice flour and cornstarch. Add liquid to dry mixture and very lightly mix together. The batter should look lumpy. Dip vegetables and seafood in tempura batter and fry in small batches until golden and crispy.

Tip

For deep-frying, peanut oil should be 2 to 3 in (5 to 7.5 cm) deep in the pot or use a deep fryer according to the manufacturer's directions.

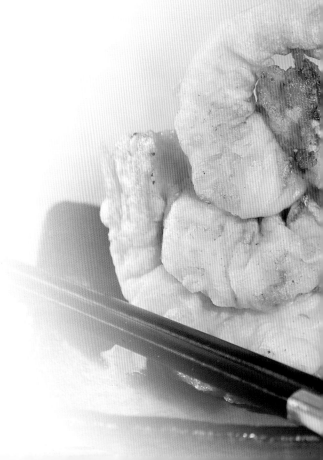

Tip

Keys to tasty, crispy tempura are a very light mixing of the batter—lumps are GOOD—and using an ice cold liquid, preferably one that is carbonated. To avoid greasy, soggy tempura, it is important to maintain the proper temperature of the oil, so it's best to have a thermometer on hand.

The word "tempura" comes from the Latin ad tempora cuaresmae, *meaning "in the time of Lent." As good Catholics, the Portuguese missionaries substituted fish for meat at this time of year, and batter-frying was a popular presentation.*

Balsamic-glazed Root Vegetables

Serves 4 as a side dish

The term "root vegetable" is used to describe all vegetables grown underground, including potatoes, carrots, onions, rutabagas and beets. Before greenhouses and imported fruits and vegetables, root vegetables were important winter food because they were easy to grow, lasted months in the cellar and were carbohydrate-dense and thus, filling. Today in British Columbia, many of the province's top chefs, who are committed to putting local produce on their tables, are finding new and creative ways to incorporate BC's great winter crop into their menus. This recipe uses the sweetness of reduced balsamic vinegar to enhance the earthy flavours of these winter staples.

Marinade

¼ cup (60 mL) balsamic vinegar

¼ cup (60 mL) extra virgin olive oil or melted butter

2 Tbsp (30 mL) honey

¼ cup (60 mL) fresh parsley, finely chopped

Root Vegetables

1 lb (500 g) baby potatoes, a variety if possible, washed and halved or quartered, depending on size

2 medium parsnips, peeled and quartered lengthwise, then halved

1 medium yam, halved and sliced ¼ in (6 mm) thick

(continued on next page)

Preheat oven to 375° F (190° C). Combine balsamic vinegar, oil, honey and parsley and set aside.

Place vegetables into a large mixing bowl. Pour prepared marinade over top, season with salt and pepper and toss to coat. Place into 13 x 9-in (33 x 23 cm) pan and assemble the rosemary and thyme sprigs on top. Roast uncovered, turning once or twice, for about 45 minutes or until edges are golden brown and vegetables pierce easily with a knife. Toss with fresh parsley and serve.

Balsamic vinegar is an aged reduction sauce that originates in the Modena region of Italy. The best balsamic vinegar is aged for a long time, comes in very small bottles and is very expensive. Instead, try a cheaper variety, but not the cheapest—it's most likely red vinegar and brown sugar or caramel.

1 small beet, washed and quartered with skin on

1 large carrot, peeled and quartered lengthwise, then halved

1 bulb garlic, broken into cloves, peeled and left whole

1 small yellow onion, peeled and quartered

sea salt and freshly ground pepper to taste

2 sprigs fresh thyme

2 sprigs fresh rosemary

Broccoli and Tempeh Rice Bowl

Serves 4

BC is one of the healthiest provinces in Canada, and we have a population that values exercise and healthy eating. This dish combines one of our favourite green vegetables with tempeh, which is similar to tofu and is a staple in many vegetarian diets. Tempeh is made in a similar fashion to tofu using soybeans, but its fermentation process is slightly different, resulting in a stronger flavour, a firmer texture and a higher content of protein, dietary fibre and vitamins. You can find tempeh at many local health food stores or even major grocers such as Whole Foods and Capers. Tempeh's firm texture makes it a good substitute for meat in many recipes.

2 Tbsp (30 mL) soy sauce

1 Tbsp (15 mL) mirin or sweet rice wine

2 Tbsp (30 mL) light miso

1 tsp (5 mL) toasted sesame oil

¼ tsp (1 mL) cornstarch

2 tsp (10 mL) grape seed or canola oil

1 Tbsp (15 mL) ginger, finely chopped

2 tsp (10 mL) lemongrass, tender bottom part only, chopped

2 cloves garlic, minced

(continued on next page)

In a small bowl, combine soy sauce, mirin, miso, sesame oil and cornstarch. Stir with a whisk and set aside. Heat grape seed or canola oil in a large skillet over medium-high and sauté ginger, lemongrass and garlic for 1 minute or just until mixture begins to brown. Add tempeh and sauté for 2 minutes, then add broccoli, peppers and snow peas and sauté for 1 minute. Add reserved mixture to skillet and cook for 1 minute, until sauce has slightly thickened. Remove from heat and stir in green onions, sesame seeds and salt. Serve over rice.

Tip

Soak your broccoli in warm, salted water to get rid of any critters. As with all members of the cabbage family, broccoli is best used within a few days of picking to retain its sweet flavour and mild odour.

🍃 Tempeh is a fermented soybean product that has been enjoyed in Southeast Asia for centuries. It is fermented with a Rhizopus mould, which makes the soy protein more easily digestible.

1 package Indonesian-style tempeh, cut into ½ in (1.25 cm) strips

1 head of broccoli, cut into florets

½ cup (125 mL) each yellow and red pepper, cut into strips

½ cup (125 mL) snow peas

½ cup (125 mL) green onions, cut in ¼ in (6 mm) diagonal strips

2 tsp (10 mL) black sesame seeds

½ tsp (2 mL) sea salt

2 cups (500 mL) hot, cooked brown rice

Apple Muffins with Ginger Glaze

Makes 12

These apple muffins pay tribute to the late Father Pandosy, an Oblate missionary who not only planted BC's first vineyard and apple orchard in Kelowna, but who also established the region's first school and Roman Catholic mission in 1860. The Okanagan Valley is still one of Canada's prime apple-growing regions; however, some people are concerned that the success of BC's wine industry could be the demise of this region's famed apples, with many farms replacing orchards with vineyards. Some of the most popular Okanagan apple varieties include Jonagold, Macintosh, Red Delicious and Spartans.

1 Jonagold or Spartan apple

2 cups (500 mL) flour

1 Tbsp (15 mL) baking powder

½ tsp (2 mL) cinnamon

¼ tsp (1 mL) salt

⅓ cup (75 mL) unsalted butter

⅓ cup (75 mL) packed brown sugar

2 eggs

⅔ cup (150 mL) buttermilk

Glaze
⅓ cup (75 mL) ginger jelly

Preheat oven to 400° F (205° C) and grease a muffin pan. Core and peel apple and cut into 1/4 in (6 mm) chunks. Into a bowl, sift together flour, baking powder, cinnamon and salt. In a saucepan, melt butter and stir in brown sugar. Remove pan from heat and let it cool slightly. Whisk eggs and buttermilk into butter mixture until smooth and add to flour mixture, stirring very lightly until combined. Fold in chunks of apple. Divide batter into muffin cups and bake for 15 minutes or until golden.

Heat ginger jelly in a small saucepan over low heat until just warm. Brush jam over muffins until absorbed for a nice glaze.

Sunflower Granola

Makes about 11½ cups (2.9 L)

The crisp, wholesome nature of granola reflects British Columbia's laid-back, outdoorsy lifestyle. What was once considered the epitome of "hippy food" in the 1960s and a snack food for hikers is now a mainstream breakfast item. A simple mixture of toasted whole grains, nuts and honey, granola can be spruced up with dried BC cranberries or blueberries. It is best eaten with yogurt while wearing cosy slippers and poring over the Saturday morning paper. The sunflower seed featured in this granola has been grown commercially in Canada since the early 1940s and is seen towering over backyards all over the province in the summer months.

4 cups (1 L) old-fashioned oats (not quick)

1 cup (250 mL) unsweetened, shredded coconut

1 cup (250 mL) dried fruit of choice: blueberries, cherries, sliced apricots, etc.

1 cup (250 mL) pumpkin seeds

1½ cups (375 mL) sunflower seeds

½ cup (125 mL) sesame seeds

1 cup (250 mL) wheat germ

1 cup (250 mL) chopped almonds

½ cup (125 mL) chopped cashews

⅔ cup (150 mL) maple syrup

1 tsp (5 mL) pure vanilla extract

½ tsp (2 mL) salt

¼ cup (60 mL) sunflower oil

Preheat oven to 325° F (160° C). Place all ingredients in a large bowl and mix well. Spread on a baking sheet and bake for 15 minutes. Stir and bake 10 more minutes. Stir again and bake 5 to 10 minutes more until golden brown. Cool and store in an airtight container for up to 1 month.

Tip

Sprinkle granola over your favourite cereal or yogurt, or simply enjoy with milk. You can also eat it plain by the handful, or you can freeze it for use at another time.

Caramel-dipped Apples

Serves 8

This recipe is inspired by summer memories of the Pacific National Exhibition (PNE), which takes places the last two weeks of August every year in Vancouver. The PNE has been a Vancouver tradition since 1910 when it was founded, and it now welcomes more than three million people every year. For many families in BC, the fair is a tradition, and each person must stop at his or her favourite food court stand, whether it be the mini-donuts, whales tails, cotton candy or caramel apples. The next time you are craving a taste of summer, try this recipe.

1 lb (500 g) dark brown sugar

¾ cup (175 mL) unsalted butter, room temperature

1 x 10 oz (300 mL) can sweetened condensed milk

⅔ cup (150 mL) light corn syrup

¼ tsp (1 mL) sea salt

1 tsp (5 mL) vanilla

¼ cup (60 mL) whipping cream

8 firm apples, such as Granny Smith, stems removed, washed and dried

8 wooden sticks, such as craft sticks or chopsticks

Combine brown sugar, butter, condensed milk, corn syrup and salt in a heavy-bottomed pot over medium-low heat and stir slowly but continually to dissolve sugar until mixture reaches a temperature between 234 and 240° F (112 and 115° C) on a candy thermometer, or soft-ball stage (see Tip, below). Remove from heat, stir in vanilla and cream and pour into a clean metal bowl. Cool until caramel is 200° F (95° C), about 15 minutes.

While caramel is cooling, line a baking sheet with buttered parchment paper and push a stick into stem end of each apple. Dip apples in caramel and let excess caramel drip off before setting on greased paper. Cool before eating. Chill any uneaten apples, wrapped in cellophane, for up to 1 week.

Tip

The soft-ball stage is a candy test in which you drop a little syrup in cold water, and as the syrup cools, it forms a soft ball that flattens when it is removed from the water.

Tip

Once the caramel apples have set, dip them into melted chocolate for an extra decadent Halloween treat. You can also roll them in chopped nuts, candy sprinkles or crushed candy bars!

Tip

If your apples are quite waxy, dip them in boiling water for 30 seconds to remove the wax. Dry very well.

Cranberry Chutney

Makes 4 cups (1 L)

Cranberries were a vital food to First Nations people and pioneers because of their naturally occurring benzoic acid, which is a great natural preservative, and their high vitamin C content. Although cranberries are thought of primarily as a Thanksgiving accompaniment, cranberry juice ranks third in sales in North America, after apple and orange. A large percentage of Canada's commercial cranberry crop is grown in southwestern BC, and it is the province's most economically important berry. Every fall, a cranberry festival is held in Fort Langley.

1 Tbsp (15 mL) unsalted butter

8 oz (250 g) pearl onions or cipollini, peeled and left whole

2 Tbsp (30 mL) grated ginger

1 serrano chili, minced

2 kaffir lime leaves or 1 Tbsp (15 mL) lime zest

2¼ cups (560 mL) apple cider vinegar

1 cup (250 mL) light brown sugar

1 cup (250 mL) muscovado sugar

2 lbs (1 kg) fresh cranberries

¾ cup (175 mL) dried fruit such as currants, cranberries, blueberries or sour cherries

sea salt and freshly ground pepper

In a medium-sized pot, melt butter and sauté onions over medium heat for 5 minutes. Add ginger, chili, lime leaves or zest, vinegar and both sugars 6 and bring to a boil. Add cranberries and dried fruit, turn heat to medium-low and simmer for about 15 minutes or until chutney is thick and has reduced.

Season with salt and pepper, and refrigerate until well chilled.

Tip

Instead of the fresh cranberries in this recipe, you could use mango, rhubarb, apple, pear or peach—or experiment using a variety of fruits.

The word "cranberry" comes from "craneberry"; the flower looks like the head of a crane, and cranes were known to enjoy the berries.

Hazelnut Torte with Okanagan Sour Cherry Preserve

Serves 10 to 12

Hazelnuts are the only nut crop commercially produced in BC, with more than 660,000 pounds (300,000 kilograms) produced annually. The majority of the province's hazelnut farms are located in the Fraser Valley, where producers press the nuts for their oil or grind them into flour as well as sell them whole. Joy Road Organics has created an Okanagan Sour Cherry Preserve that is one of the best in the province, using organically grown cherries from the Naramata Bench region. With its pure, syrupy flavour, this preserve is a fantastic contrast to the hazelnut torte. By combining these two unique ingredients, you have a truly BC dessert!

2 cups (500 mL) cake flour

2 tsp (10 mL) baking powder

½ tsp (2 mL) salt

6 egg yolks

½ cup (125 mL) canola oil

½ cup (125 mL) water

1 cup (250 mL) sugar

6 egg whites

1 cup (250 mL) hazelnuts, chopped and toasted

¼ cup (60 mL) strong brewed coffee, cooled

(continued on next page)

Preheat oven to 350° F (175° C). Grease and lightly flour two 9 in (23 cm) springform pans. Combine flour, baking powder and salt in a bowl and set aside. In a large mixing bowl, beat egg yolks, oil, water and sugar with an electric mixer on medium speed for 5 minutes, scraping bowl occasionally. Fold in flour mixture.

In another large mixing bowl, beat egg whites with an electric mixer on medium to high speed until soft peaks form. Gently fold about 1 cup (250 mL) of egg white mixture into egg yolk mixture. Fold rest of the egg yolk mixture into remaining egg white mixture. Then fold in chopped hazelnuts. Spoon batter evenly into prepared pans. Bake in oven for 20 minutes or until a toothpick inserted in centre comes out clean. Immediately poke holes all over both cakes with a toothpick and drizzle coffee evenly over. Let cakes cool on wire racks for 10 minutes before removing from pans. When they have cooled completely, slice in half horizontally.

For all types of nuts, a 3.5 oz (100 g) serving has 550 to 700 calories and contains protein, phosphorus and potassium.

In a medium saucepan, heat cream to simmer. Remove from heat and add bittersweet chocolate, stirring until melted. Reserve ¼ cup (60 mL) of chocolate mixture for drizzling; cover and set aside. Cool remaining chocolate mixture to room temperature, about an hour.

Transfer mixture to a medium bowl and beat with an electric mixer on medium speed for about 3 minutes, until it has thickened. Spread chocolate filling evenly on 3 cake layers, and frost top and sides with chocolate hazelnut spread. Drizzle the reserved chocolate mixture on top and garnish with toasted hazelnuts. Serve with sour cherry preserve on side.

1 cup (250 mL) heavy cream (32%)

6 oz (170 g) bittersweet chocolate, chopped

1 x 14 oz (400 g) jar of Nutella chocolate hazelnut spread

toasted hazelnuts

1 x 8 oz (250 mL) jar of sour cherry preserve

Index

About the Authors

Eric Pateman, president and founder of Edible Canada, has worked in the hospitality industry for over 20 years both as a chef and a hotel consultant, and he has rated restaurants for the Mobil Travel Guide. Eric's travels have taken him throughout North America and to the United Kingdom and Africa, where he has sought out unique culinary experiences. He was named as one of Business in Vancouver's Top 40 Under 40 Business People in 2007, and to Western Living Magazine's list of the Top 40 Foodies Under 40 in Western Canada in 2008. He lives in Squamish with his favourite leading ladies—his wife and two daughters.

Canadian chef **Jennifer Ogle** learned her craft from a variety of sources, among them the renowned French cooking school La Varenne, which lead to an opportunity to work in the Michelin-starred restaurant La Madeleine in Burgundy, France. Jennifer recalls that her love of cooking started at an early age, when many Sunday afternoons were spent experimenting in the kitchen. Today, Jennifer enjoys all aspects of the culinary world, from cooking to writing, with a particular passion for seasonal, local ingredients.

James Darcy is a self-confessed epicure whose food and travel interests have taken him around the world. A dedicated researcher into food and culinary techniques, he is also passionate about food folklore.

Jean Paré started her official culinary career as a caterer in Vermilion, Alberta, before going on to found Company's Coming and become Canada's most popular cookbook author—selling 30 million books! Her story appears on p. 4.